BRIDGEPORT
Tales from
THE PARK CITY

ERIC D. LEHMAN

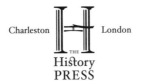

Charleston · London
THE History PRESS

Published by The History Press
Charleston, SC 29403
www.historypress.net

Copyright © 2009 by Eric D. Lehman
All rights reserved

First published 2009

Manufactured in the United States

ISBN 978.1.59629.616.9

Library of Congress Cataloging-in-Publication Data

Lehman, Eric D.
Bridgeport : tales from the park city / Eric D. Lehman.
p. cm.
Includes bibliographical references.
ISBN 978-1-59629-616-9
1. Bridgeport (Conn.)--History--Anecdotes. 2. Bridgeport (Conn.)--Biography--Anecdotes. I. Title.
F104.B7L44 2009
974.6'9--dc22
2009002885

Notice: The information in this book is true and complete to the best of our knowledge. It is offered without guarantee on the part of the author or The History Press. The author and The History Press disclaim all liability in connection with the use of this book.

All rights reserved. No part of this book may be reproduced or transmitted in any form whatsoever without prior written permission from the publisher except in the case of brief quotations embodied in critical articles and reviews.

At the end of an hour we saw a far-away town sleeping in a valley by a winding river; and beyond it on a hill, a vast gray fortress, with towers and turrets, the first I had ever seen out of a picture.
"Bridgeport?" said I, pointing.
"Camelot," said he.
—*Mark Twain,* A Connecticut Yankee in King Arthur's Court

CONTENTS

	Prologue	7
Chapter 1	A World in Miniature	10
Chapter 2	Stitching History	22
Chapter 3	Lincoln's First Fried Oyster	30
Chapter 4	With Her Eyes to the Sea	39
Chapter 5	When Animals Roamed the Streets	47
Chapter 6	The Playthings of Possibility	58
Chapter 7	Becoming Park City	68
Chapter 8	A Tale of Two Inventors	77
Chapter 9	Textbooks and Toothaches	86
Chapter 10	Arsenal of a Nation	95
Chapter 11	The *Pogo* Years	105
Chapter 12	Tragedy and Rebirth	113
	Bibliography	119
	About the Author	127

PROLOGUE

As the Marquis de Lafayette reined in at Knapp's Hotel in 1824, he barely recognized the town in the summer darkness. When he had last ridden through the unpainted village fifty years earlier with General George Washington, a single-track King's Highway wound its solitary way around salt marshes. The name Stratfield had marked the territory then. Now, the inhabitants of the small cluster of houses on the Pequonnock River called their borough Bridgeport. Brightly decorated homes coupled along two main streets, providing a much easier passage for the aging marquis. America was growing, and Lafayette marveled at its eagerness to embrace new possibilities.

The town still followed the lead of its immediate neighbors, Fairfield and Stratford, both of which had been important in the War for Independence. Lafayette knew that his comrade, Washington, had trotted through here several times during the Revolution. The old warhorse had spoken of good refreshment at Nichols' Tavern. But the hour was already eleven o'clock, and Lafayette had arrived too late to take part in the celebration prepared for him. He withdrew to bed in a back room and promptly fell asleep.

In the morning, Bridgeport's famed visitor woke abruptly to the sound of a dozen drums outside Knapp's. After dressing and refreshing himself, he received town elders Mr. Hubbell and Mr. Lockwood, and the three of them appeared on the hotel balcony at the corner of Wall and Water Streets. The walkway by the brick storefronts swarmed with ladies wearing their finest hats, while their husbands gallantly took to the dusty August street. The town had suffered smallpox outbreaks during the Revolution, and grim pockmarks were still evident on the older faces. Three cheers rang out from the crowd, stirring the hero to response: "I am very happy to receive your kind welcome." They cheered loudly but quieted when he spoke again. With a voice full of emotion, no doubt thinking of this vast country and the love its people had shown him, he said softly, "Happy, happy people!"

Prologue

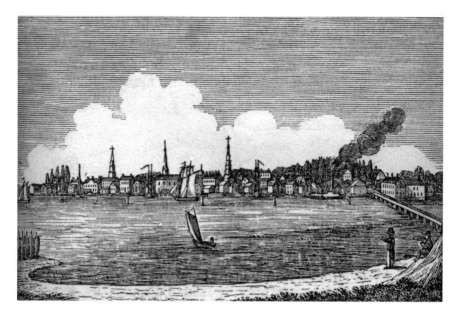

J.W. Barber's 1837 drawing captures the busy town of Bridgeport only one year after being chartered. *Courtesy of Bridgeport Public Library Historical Collections.*

Though he had not eaten breakfast, the elderly French general shook hands with each of the ladies, and then, one by one, with the men of Bridgeport. They welcomed him merrily to their new town with quite a bit of hometown pride. He didn't know it, but the modest Knapp's Hotel had witnessed similar commotion when it hosted a ball at the end of the War of 1812, capping off a parade held to applaud the peace between Britain and America. Finally, the line of well-wishers and admirers stopped, and Lafayette went inside to devour a full brunch. He had a long way to go yet to meet his old friend John Adams in Boston.

As the party mounted their horses and began to jog down the packed earth of the highway, a chaotic procession of horses and carriages scrambled into a procession behind him. The motley crew of townspeople cheered the marquis, clearly believing themselves to be some sort of escort. Finally, General Enoch Foote made an official statement of farewell, but a few of these persistent devotees kept to the rear of the party all the way to the edge of New Haven.

Lafayette did not foresee it, but this small town would become a center of creative industry and would one day evolve to be the largest city in Connecticut. Its people would watch the sea and take to the sky. Its inventors would transform the fields of metalwork, sewing and dental hygiene. There

Prologue

would be famous colonels and famous cartoonists. Two of its citizens would go on to become the most popular entertainers of the nineteenth century. Thousands of others would help America win both world wars. But first, those people needed a little elbow room. Twelve years after the famous hero of the Revolution passed through Bridgeport, the townsfolk asked for a charter from the State of Connecticut. They would become their own city at last and live proudly in the inspired vanguard of the possible.

Chapter 1

A WORLD IN MINIATURE

In November 1842, the Hudson River at Albany froze over, and a frustrated P.T. Barnum wearily decided to take the train home. When the train stopped in Bridgeport, he stepped out to spend the night in the newly painted Franklin House, which his half brother Philo managed. That night, he heard the people at the hotel mention that Bridgeport boasted the smallest boy alive. Asking Philo to find this wonder, Barnum ate a leisurely dinner at the hotel. By the dessert course, the diminutive Charles Stratton toddled into the dining room for what was surely one of the most fateful meetings of two entertainers in American history.

Phineas T. Barnum was born in Bethel during an age when pigs roamed the streets freely and peddlers from nearby Bridgeport drove carts full of fish and clams to the small town. As a young man, he had offered a sweepstakes scheme there, proposing better odds than the state lottery, until the government outlawed it in 1833. Undeterred, he had opened a fruit and confectionary store, sold books and married a tailoress named Charity Hallett. He also established a weekly newspaper called the *Herald of Freedom*, which landed him in jail for libel. Of course, this only increased the subscriptions to his newspaper, and his release from the Danbury jail was the occasion of a massive celebration that included sixty carriages and forty horsemen ushering him home to Bethel while a band trumpeted victory. The youthful businessman never forgot the power of this spectacle to win people's hearts and minds.

This incident may have prompted Barnum's true calling. Shortly thereafter, he heard the story of Joyce Heth, supposedly 161 years old and the former nurse to George Washington, and quickly contrived to sign as her manager. He arranged for the exhibition of this partially paralyzed but spirited old slave and began a publicity campaign. She answered questions about Washington and the Revolutionary War with aplomb and

Tales from the Park City

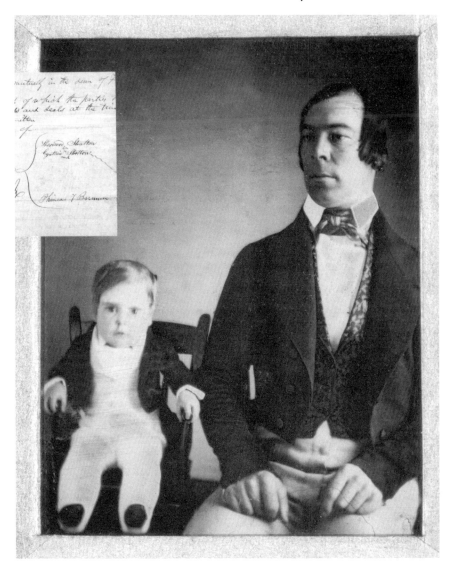

An 1842 photograph of Charles Stratton at age four. At two feet high, the boy would only grow a few more inches. *Courtesy of the Barnum Museum, Bridgeport, CT.*

confidence. After a time displaying jugglers, acting as agent for dancers and selling Bibles, Barnum returned to New York and opened his famous American Museum. But he needed a starring act to bring in the crowds.

And now here stood Charles Sherwood Stratton, a showman's dream. In November 1842, the four-year-old boy was only twenty-five inches high and weighed only fifteen pounds. Charles had been born a healthy child at nine

BRIDGEPORT

pounds and two ounces. However, his development seemed unfortunately slow. In his promotion for "General Tom Thumb," Barnum stated, "Although in every other respect he grew day by day, with great rapidity, never a hair's breadth more was added to his length. No longer, no shorter, no heavier, but much handsomer, a great deal shapelier, and considerable stronger." A faulty pituitary gland caused Charles to keep this very small size but left him without bodily deformities. In fact, the boy from Bridgeport was quite striking, with fair hair and complexion. Barnum described him as having "fresh, rosy cheeks, large beautiful dark eyes, a fine forehead, a handsome mouth, and great vivacity of expression and hilarity of manner."

When Charles was born in 1838, the town itself was hardly over a year old. The mud-covered streets bogged down carriages and gravel sidewalks stretched only in front of rich homes and city buildings. Open sewers provided scant drainage and the pipes for city water consisted of little more than hollowed logs. Trading eggs or beans for flour or nails remained a suitable practice, cash not being acceptable in some stores. Cows strayed from their pastures and wandered the streets. This was a town far behind its neighbors in many ways.

Still, an urgent sense of life brewed here. Wagons and carts jammed the streets downtown, full of provisions and dry goods picked up from the wharves. Men strolling the streets wore high silk beaver hats, long coats and kipskin boots. Women in ribboned bonnets and festooned skirts greeted them with hands protected by horseskin gloves. In the evening, whale oil lamps provided dim lights for the busy citizens. Night watches roamed the dark alleys to keep order. New industries of saddlery, carriage building and coffin making marked the city's growth, as did the daily steamship to New York City.

But Bridgeport had a long way to go. In the 1830s, three hundred white pine clapboard houses and a few dozen stores were not impressive for New England. Living in the north end of this city, Charles's father, Sherwood, found work as a poor carpenter and his mother, Cynthia, waitressed at a nearby inn. Neither expressed happiness with their son, and in fact Sherwood was "ashamed." Barnum took them in with a less than generous contract—three dollars a week plus room and board—and spirited the dazed family from their humble, dirt-floored home.

They found themselves in a stranger land than expected, working in the carnival atmosphere of Barnum's American Museum. Exhibits ranged widely, from "petrified" pork to a portion of the throne of Louis XVIII. Here the tiny, juvenile Charles transformed into "General Tom Thumb." Both children and adults were delighted by Charles's perfect proportions, calling him a "man in miniature." This became a huge selling point for Barnum as he took the show on the road, and it never disappointed viewers. Biographies, lithographs and other pamphlets were distributed wherever they went, a tactic that Barnum pioneered to set the stage for grand entrances. While traveling, impersonations quickly became the clear hits for Charles. He dressed in Yankee Doodle suits, Cupid outfits and Napoleon uniforms. Occasionally, he fought pretend battles with Barnum's seven-foot-high "giants," playing the part of David to their Goliaths. Barnum himself quickly grew fond of the young boy and began to think of him as more than just an employee.

For his part, Charles was eager to learn the acts that his new mentor prepared for him and memorized scripts and affects that might have stumped older actors. Sometimes Barnum set the stage with miniature furniture or a toy house. He often brought Charles to the stage in a tiny wooden carriage, barely three feet high, with plush red interior and "Tom Thumb" painted on the door. "Tom" would leap out with a tiny stovepipe hat and marble-topped bamboo cane, causing gasps of astonishment. In the act he would often sing a song to the tune of "Yankee Doodle," which began, "I'm General Thumb, just come to town, Yankee Doodle Dandy…" At a dinner with a newspaper editor, "Tom Thumb" stood on the table to carve a turkey, which the guests were assured weighed more than he did. He kicked over a glass of water, telling the group that he didn't want to fall in. Barnum often appeared as a straight man during these sketches and skits, and the two developed a quick repartee that involved Barnum setting Charles up for the punch lines of jokes. His gleeful attitude and proud strutting before audiences changed their feelings from sympathy to wonder. It was clear that this little Bridgeporter had a genius for showmanship to rival his boss. Barnum raised his salary to seven dollars a week.

Charles returned to New York and the American Museum, where he relaxed a little after the demanding performance schedules of a tour. Taking the train, he often went back to Bridgeport, finding fewer peddlers selling tinware and more brick buildings going up. The Pequonnock tribe had seemingly disappeared from Golden Hill, but hundreds of immigrants had arrived from Ireland. Several whaling companies had been successful, but the toll-taking turnpike companies were losing importance. Bridgeport seemed small now to the still diminutive Charles, but it was home.

Meanwhile, to try to shore up falling profits, Barnum staged a buffalo hunt in Hoboken, New Jersey, that ended with the animals fleeing into a swamp. A faked mermaid nearly cost him any reputation he had left for reliability. Luckily, he still had the loyalty of Charles Stratton, and they decided on

BRIDGEPORT

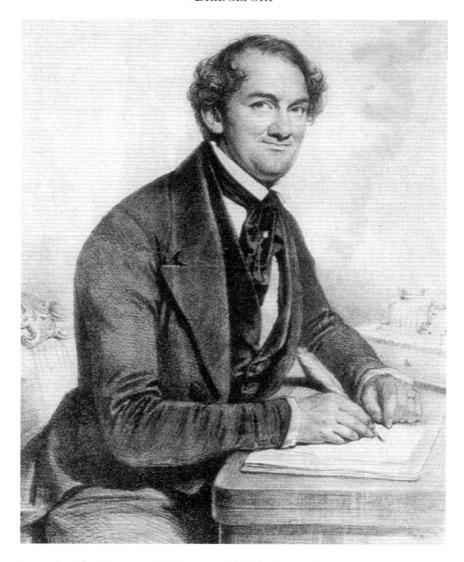

A rare drawing of the young P.T. Barnum at his desk. *Courtesy of the Barnum Museum, Bridgeport, CT.*

a European tour. When they reached London, the American minister promised to get them in to see Queen Victoria. Charles, dressed in a tight white vest, buttoned pants and a black Prince Albert coat, complete with tiny epaulets on his shoulders, charmed her. He fought with the queen's poodle and created a hilarious exit, combining court decorum with frantic action. This seemingly underprivileged boy from Bridgeport made everyone fans of his humor and talent. When the Duke of Wellington paid the six-year-old boy a visit, he found Charles sitting thoughtfully in his Napoleon outfit. The duke asked him what he was thinking, and the small wonder said, "I was thinking of the loss of the Battle of Waterloo." Had Stratton rehearsed this in advance or did he find true comic inspiration? With Barnum as his mentor, it was impossible to tell.

Finally, in 1845, as "General Tom Thumb" wooed the citizens of Britain and Ireland, the Strattons negotiated a better contract with Barnum, splitting the proceeds of Charles's appearances with the promoter. Unfortunately, the money went to the heads of these uncomplicated Bridgeporters, and they quickly put on airs. Barnum stated in a letter that "Bridgeport will be quite too small to hold him [Sherwood] on our return, and as for his wife, she will look upon New York or Boston as dirty villages, quite beneath her notice." They also began demanding to control their son more and more. With a businessman's expertise, Barnum crushed them and threatened to stop the entire affair. Luckily for Charles, these early celebrity parents retreated. There was no love lost between the parties, though, and Charles himself no doubt felt torn between the parents who had once despised him and this new father figure.

Paris was next for this young Bridgeport boy and his meteoric rise to fame. After visits to the royal family, at which he played Napoleon to rousing approbation, he toured France and Europe for two more years. French children were encouraged to come onstage to compare their heights with "Tom Thumb" and Charles suffered, to his great delight, kisses from thousands of "pretty ladies." Back in England, Charles escaped death when a horse stampeded into a stone wall. The carriage was smashed to bits, but fortunately their escort grabbed Charles and leaped over the wall just as the carriage crashed, preserving both their lives. However, this hinted to both Barnum and Charles that it was time to go home.

On Barnum's return from Europe, Walt Whitman interviewed him for the *Brooklyn Eagle*. The unknown poet asked Barnum if the journey had made him love America less. "No! Not a bit of it! Why, sir, you can't imagine the difference. There, everything is frozen—kings and things—formal, but absolutely frozen, here it is life. Here it is freedom, and here are men." Whitman was impressed, saying, "A whole book might be written on that little speech of Barnum's." No doubt it is a coincidence, but a few years later Whitman would write his masterwork *Leaves of Grass* on those very themes, and it would become the most famous American book of poetry in the nineteenth century.

With the profits from his exploits, Charles's parents built a large house in north Bridgeport, with a separate apartment scaled to Charles's size. They also had the money to buy gorgeous, specially made furniture to fill it. They received P.T. Barnum there, and together appraised the changes that had come to the city. Having grown up in nearby Bethel, Barnum was no stranger to Bridgeport. However, since he had taken the young Charles Stratton from his home, the showman had been focusing on traveling the world with his acts and setting up his American Museum in New York City. Living in hotels began to wear on him. During the European tours, he decided to build a permanent home and now decided on the Strattons' own town. He loved the picturesque setting on Long Island Sound, and the new railroads allowed him easy access to New York. Impressed by the royal pavilion at Brighton, England, he commissioned drawings of it and designed his mansion on seventeen acres of land near the border of Fairfield. He would call the new home his "oriental palace," or Iranistan.

The house became a wonder of New England. Three stories high, the mansion had a striking appearance, with minarets and carved satyrs leading the eye up to a central, onion-shaped dome that was a full ninety

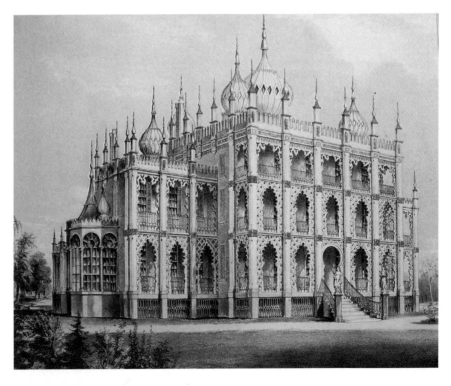

P.T. Barnum's eye for spectacle influenced the design of Iranistan, his first and most magnificent residence. *Courtesy of the Barnum Museum, Bridgeport, CT.*

feet in the air. The gardens contained orchards of orange and lemon trees, a jet-powered fountain and an artificial pond splashing with swans and eider ducks. The lavish interior included rosewood, marble, velvet and lace. Wandering from the great central hall into the seemingly endless corridors, you could find yourself in a dining room with seating for forty, a frescoed library, a billiard room or an octagonal greenhouse. Barnum installed all the newest technologies, including burglar alarms, hot and cold running water, fire alarms and a hot air heating system. It was considered, if not the largest, then the most fabulous home in all the United States. Famous singer Jenny Lind came to the United States to tour under Barnum's management solely because she had seen a picture of this amazing house on his personal stationery.

Barnum had brought Charles to New York and beyond, and now Charles had brought his mentor to Bridgeport. However, Barnum had not completed these new experiments in entertainment. During the late 1840s and early 1850s, he turned to legitimate drama for a time, showing "morality plays" in his new theatre. Following this success, he wooed Jenny Lind, the "Swedish Nightingale," to America for a singing tour. "Lindomania" followed, and she sold out concert halls in all the major cities, performing in front of President Millard Fillmore, Daniel Webster and the entire Supreme Court. No one remained immune to Barnum's hype, and none went away disappointed.

On May 12, 1856, the now teenage Charles Stratton wrote to Barnum to suggest they start a new European tour, twelve years after the first one. Charles hardly needed the money, but Barnum did. A merger with Bridgeport's Jerome Clock Company had proved disastrous, forcing the great showman into bankruptcy. They escaped his creditors and fled to England. This time Charles posed as Robinson Crusoe and a Scottish highlander. He adopted fancy court costume, cross-dressed as "Mary Ann" and impersonated famous figures such as Romulus, Samson or Cain. Due to its rousing success, the two Bridgeporters made back Barnum's fortune. During the trip he also wrote a small book called *The Art of Money-Getting*, which, fittingly, made him thousands of dollars.

During these troubles, Philo had telegrammed his brother and told him the bad news: a careless worker's cigarette had burned Iranistan to the ground. So, on his return to Bridgeport, Barnum built a new mansion called Lindencroft on the spacious property. It lacked the matchless architecture of Iranistan, but was still a fine home, considered one of Bridgeport's best. Charles invested in real estate with his former employer, buying land in East Bridgeport on which to build houses. He bought a yacht to sail in Long Island Sound and thoroughbred horses to breed. He imported expensive

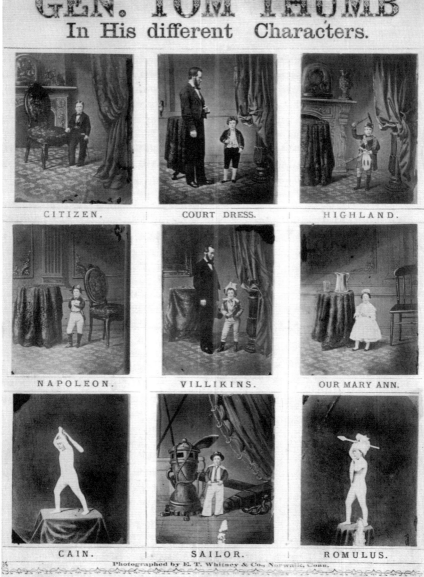

The diminutive Stratton wowed audiences playing various roles, including Romulus, Napoleon and "Mary Ann." *Courtesy of the Barnum Museum, Bridgeport, CT.*

cigars. Charles stood a full two feet, nine inches tall now, and had grown a substantial mustache. It was a good life for a poor boy from the wrong side of town.

Meanwhile, Lavinia Warren Bump was growing up in Middleborough, Massachusetts, the unusually tiny child of two large parents. At twenty-one years old, she reached only thirty-two inches high when Barnum hired her. She had been a schoolteacher and had been "displayed" once before, on a Mississippi River floating theatre. Already admired for her exquisite, dainty beauty, when she came to New York she found admirers in General Grant and Stephen A. Douglas, the candidate for president who lost to Lincoln. The famously short senator tried to kiss her, but she spurned him, primly showing him the back of her white ermine cape.

Charles saw her and fell in love immediately with her dark, wavy hair, huge liquid eyes and classically sculptured features. Lavinia was electrified by this famous man, who had met kings and queens and performed before half the world. He ferried her from New York to Bridgeport with Barnum, who took them to Lindencroft in his beautiful carriage attended by a smartly attired coachman. Then Charles took Lavinia for a drive, showing her East Bridgeport, pointing out all the houses he owned in the developments. She seemed especially impressed with the miniature apartments at his parents' house. During lunch at Lindencroft, Lavinia remarked, "Mr. Barnum or Tom Thumb own about all Bridgeport."

What woman could resist this display? Charles had learned well how to prime an audience before a performance. That evening, Charles wooed Lavinia with promises to take her to Europe. She consented and they were engaged. Only afterward did he ask her parents for permission. "Ever since I met your daughter…I have felt that kind heaven designed her for my partner in life…I assure you that if she becomes my wife, I shall always do all in my power to make her happy."

Their marriage turned into the event of the year. Barnum footed the bill, but it certainly didn't hurt his pocketbook. The museum made piles of money from the publicity surrounding the event. A Fifth Avenue store displayed Lavinia's bridal gown in the window for weeks before the ceremony. Barnum did toy with the idea of charging money for entry to a huge wedding ceremony in the Academy of Music in New York but settled on Manhattan's Grace Episcopal Church and an unusually temperate ceremony. Charles wore full evening dress, and Lavinia a gown of white satin with a diamond necklace and lace veil that matched a star-shaped bouquet. Charles also cut his dignified mustache pencil-thin for the wedding, even though Lavinia's mother tried to get him to remove it completely.

Bridgeport

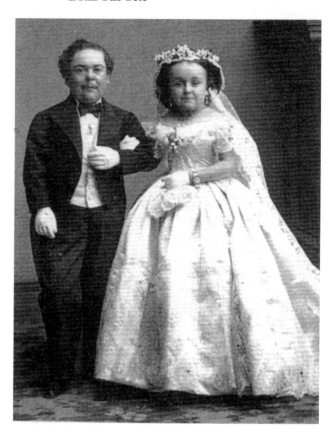

Two thousand eager guests attended the spectacular 1863 wedding of Charles Stratton and Lavinia Warren. *Courtesy of the Barnum Museum, Bridgeport, CT.*

Everyone who was anyone in New York attended Charles's wedding, standing on their pews to get a better look at the tapestried platform. The minister who had baptized Charles in Bridgeport assisted in the sacrament. Famous photographer Matthew Brady took the wedding photographs at his studio nearby and the reception was held at the Metropolitan Hotel. The newlyweds received all two thousand guests while standing on the lid of a grand piano.

By this time, Charles and his new wife could take either the railroad or steamship home to Bridgeport. It was a different place than he had been born in. By order of law, no one was allowed to keep large stores of gunpowder, and indiscriminate pistol shooting had been banned. Rubbish was kept off the new sidewalks, cows roaming the streets were impounded and piles of lumber and firewood were cleared from the muddy streets. The townspeople had even begun to get used to the strange gas lamps that lit the streets and hotel rooms. Like Charles Stratton, the city of Bridgeport started small but was quickly becoming wealthy, distinguished and important.

Tales from the Park City

In 1869, the famous couple prepared to tour the world on a voyage that would last three years and log 55,487 miles, with 1,471 shows for 587 cities and towns in places like Japan, China, Indonesia, Australia, India, Ceylon, Arabia and Egypt. Barnum would take no money from his former employees for this. He told them, "I feel as if I had no right to my share of the profit from the voyages. But don't thank me; you could easily have thrown the old man overboard long ago as thousands would have done, but I honor you for your friendship and fidelity to me. God bless you for it." As Barnum took Charles's and Lavinia's hands before they left, the greatest showman on earth had tears in his eyes.

Chapter 2

STITCHING HISTORY

Bridgeport's destiny as an industrial center was a long way off in 1730, when Richard Nichols opened his little shop on the Pequonnock River. The pastoral beauty of the rolling green hills provided a fine spot for his small wharf, warehouse and shipyard. His Berkshire Mill Pond stood nearly alone until shortly before the Revolutionary War, when Stephen Burroughs began conducting a grain trade with Boston and the West Indies. In 1790, immigrants began to settle the open fields, becoming joiners, blacksmiths and cabinetmakers. Samuel Porter opened a small weaver's "factory" on Main Street. He and his son worked hard making blankets to sell to the nearby towns. Most of the "industry" of the town was of this modest sort, assembling necessities like casks, hats and barrels, until after the War of 1812.

Isaac Sherman Sr., unrelated to the identically named first mayor, began the next major industry, a saltworks. The windmill-powered factory pumped salt water from the harbor into evaporating vats. After this experiment small industries flooded in: saddle boxes for packing saddle equipment in 1815, combs in 1830 and patent leather in 1845. Carriage making and saddlery took off, with numerous competing companies fighting for buyers across New England. But soon the radical invention of the sewing machine would launch Bridgeport as a world leader of industry.

Elias Howe invented the first truly functioning sewing machine and patented it in 1846. As a boy, he helped his father with chores on the farm and at a gristmill. At age sixteen, he snatched up a job as a machinist's apprentice, first at a local textile mill and then at a cotton mill in Lowell, Massachusetts. After becoming a full machinist, he married and promptly fathered three children. Apprenticing in a shop in Cambridge that made watches and scientific instruments, he began to tinker with a "sewing machine." These machines were not unknown in the 1840s, but no one had ever produced one that actually worked correctly, accurately or consistently.

Tales from the Park City

Howe invented a machine that used a needle with an eye at its sharp point. This device pushed thread through a piece of cloth, allowing a threaded arm to enter the loop created. As the needle drew the thread back up, it was pulled tight to create the "lock stitch." When Howe made the trip to Washington, D.C., to patent the machine, he demonstrated it to eager and fascinated crowds. It was judged the most "beautiful" and efficient machine of its time. The lockstitch mechanism went through 250 stitches per minute, the rate of five of the fastest hand sewers Howe could find. But he could not figure out how to make a profit with it and abandoned the project to try his luck in England.

Others took it up. A young cabinetmaker named Allen B. Wilson won a bronze medal at the Massachusetts Charitable Mechanics Exhibition in 1850 for his own sewing contraption. The machine was full of new and interesting features, like the rotary hook shuttle. He also perfected the two-motion feed mechanism, by which the user could control the direction of stitching. This breakthrough that Howe failed to include was vital and created the capability of changing the direction of a seam. Now, the user could stitch a continuous seam of varying angles or curves without unhooking the fabric and starting over. Eventually, he would adapt this to the four-motion feed that is still used today. Wilson received his own patents on these innovations to the machine and began to demonstrate it to fascinated observers, as Howe had done a few years earlier.

One of Wilson's machines was demonstrated in New York City, where carriage manufacturer Nathaniel Wheeler saw it. He immediately proposed a farsighted endeavor, asking Wilson to go into business with him. A deal was struck for five hundred machines to be built and the inventor earned the title of superintendent of the firm. Overseeing the production of the invention, Wilson made improvements, while the manufacturer pitched it to both factories and families. When it became clear that these odd machines would be marketable, Wheeler made Wilson a full partner.

Not everyone praised these newfangled sewing machines. Some saw them as evil monsters that would take jobs away from skilled seamstresses and tailors. Wheeler and Wilson thought differently. The legions of workers slaving away in sewing factories were underpaid and miserable. Their machine would increase output by a huge margin and give each seamstress a better life. The partners published an article that gave very convincing statistics: "A gentleman's shirt required one hour and sixteen minutes by machine and fourteen hours and twenty-six minutes by hand. A chemise, one hour and one minute by machine and ten hours and thirty-one minutes by hand." It was hard to argue with such a stark distinction.

Bridgeport

To promote the machine, Wheeler took it to O.F. Winchester, the owner of Winchester Repeating Arms Company in New Haven, which at that time manufactured shirts. At first Winchester refused to try the machine, but then he was presented with a fine shirt sewn on it by Mrs. Wilson. In light of this evidence, Winchester converted and bought the rights to sell the machine in New Haven. Now Wheeler and Wilson had a buyer, but one problem confronted the partners' grand schemes: their Watertown, Connecticut factory was small. But P.T. Barnum's failed partnership with the Jerome Clock Factory had left an empty building on the broad peninsula of East Bridgeport. Wheeler and Wilson snatched it up. They would employ over one thousand people and would help entice residents to settle the flourishing area.

Meanwhile, other changes were taking place in Bridgeport that guaranteed its relevance in the rapidly changing world. In 1836, the same year Bridgeport became its own city, the Housatonic Railroad was chartered to build a line from the new town along the meandering Housatonic River Valley. This did not please the turnpike companies, which had controlled trade and traffic through a series of toll roads. The Newtown and Bridgeport Turnpike Company would be hardest hit by the railroad, and its officers

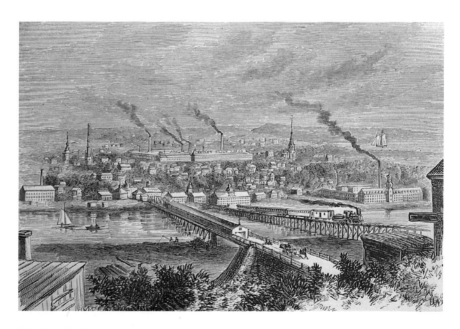

The growth of industry in East Bridgeport brings a new sight to the landscape: smoke bellowing from the Wheeler and Wilson factory. *Courtesy of the Barnum Museum, Bridgeport, CT.*

signed petitions, hired lawyers and presented their case to the people of Bridgeport. However, they were fighting a futile battle against the mighty iron road of the future.

Workers completed the line to New Milford by 1840 and continued to lay tracks through the sugarloaf hills of northwest Connecticut. The *Bridgeport Standard* reported that on February 11, 1840, the first train, decorated with flags, left the city at nine o'clock in the morning to a rousing concert by the Bridgeport Band. The schedule was timed to coincide with the steamboat arrivals and departures from New York, eventually making Bridgeport an important stopping point on the way to the mines and factories of Pittsfield in the Berkshires.

At first, the small engines shot sparks from their wood-burning stacks, often spattering angry passengers. Small fires sometimes broke out in the coach cars, where customers sat on hard, flat boards. Smoke and dust choked them constantly. Stops were jerky and jolting, as engineers used either clunky foot brakes or actually stuck chunks of wood into the train wheel spokes. The original track curled up slightly with the weight of the train, causing spikes to pop up. A workman in the caboose with a hammer would tap them down as the train chugged past.

Nevertheless, the Housatonic Railroad continued to expand throughout the prewar years, crisscrossing the river valleys and rocky hills of western Connecticut and Massachusetts. The iron, granite, marble and lime quarries of the Berkshires and Litchfield Hills used the railroad to send raw materials to the processors in New York. A train called the "Milk Train" or "Big Milk" began chugging downstate from Pittsfield, picking up milk along the way and arriving at Bridgeport with thirty carloads of the precious commodity. In 1849, the New York and New Haven Railroad also opened, with a depot at Bridgeport across from the Atlantic Hotel. Most importantly, linking this rail system to its port created a nexus of activity and allowed the new city to begin to eclipse its neighbors, Fairfield and Stratford.

However, not everything went well at first. The section of the city known as East Bridgeport essentially seceded from the town over the issue of taxes. The city elders pointed out that the small neck of land shared in plenty of the advantages and should shoulder some of the burden. Nevertheless, the city limits were altered, and it was not until 1864 that these two sections would truly be joined again. Meanwhile, tragedy changed the location of the downtown when an oyster saloon on Bank Street caught fire. The resulting conflagration burned down most of the Water Street business district in 1845.

The air crackled on that cold December night, and the firemen with their signature white wands dashed to their engines in heavy coats. But the fire had broken out at low tide, preventing the nearly frozen fire engines from pumping any water from the Pequonnock River. The pipes jammed with mud, the firemen despaired and forty-nine buildings went up in an inferno. Molasses barrels unloaded from West Indies ships exploded and drenched the docks in sticky goo. Firefighters fought valiantly to prevent the flames from reaching Main Street by covering the side of the connecting building in wet carpets. This unusual strategy worked, and the merchants who had not lost everything dejectedly rebuilt in this salvaged area.

The growing population encountered another serious problem when the drinking water ran out. A few public wells and a spring on Golden Hill offered barely enough, and when dry years came, people suffered. The council fiddled with the idea of a reservoir but instead gave the problem to Nathaniel Green of Pequonnock Mills in the north of the city. Now in control of the newly formed Bridgeport Water Company, Green laid pipes along the city streets, installed hydrants and charged businesses and the public for their water. This outlandish idea was an anathema to ordinary citizens, but they soon got used to it, having little choice in the matter.

Bridges were built, including the vital Center Bridge, a draw that charged tolls and connected the peninsula of East Bridgeport to Gold Street downtown. It allowed an entirely new community to travel and trade quite easily, rather than cross the water miles up the Pequonnock River. Financial services for the growing trade could also now be handled by a local bank. It had originally opened as the Bridgeport Savings Bank, but in 1842 the People's Bank began to take deposits. The city also became a center of judicial affairs for the county in 1853, when the General Assembly stated that "from and after the first day of October next, the Supreme court of Errors, the Superior court and the County court in the county of Fairfield" should be held in Bridgeport.

With the infrastructure in place, production at the Wheeler and Wilson factory soared. Hundreds of buyers in New York and New England willingly invested in this fresh technology. Always looking forward, Wheeler took out patents for a variety of inventions in numerous fields: power transmitters, wood filling compounds, refrigerators, ventilation systems and of course sewing machine improvements. But the two partners were in for a fight. On his return from several years in England, Elias Howe saw this triumphant success and sued Wilson and all the other infringers for his rightful royalties.

Howe struggled for years in this bitter patent battle, focusing his official ire on the more famous Isaac Singer, whom he saw as his primary adversary. Eventually, a judge's decision gave Howe control of the entire market and

Tales from the Park City

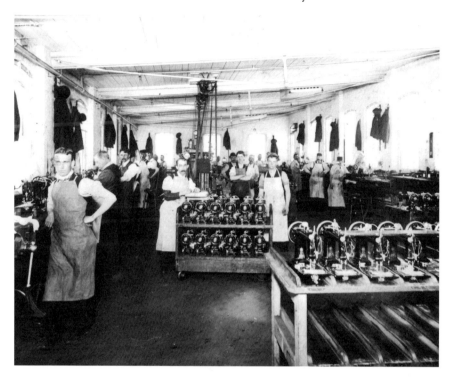

The sewing machine makes Bridgeport a key player in the Industrial Revolution. Workers at Wheeler and Wilson ready the appliances for sale. *Courtesy of the Bridgeport Public Library Historical Collections.*

granted him royalties from Singer and all others making a profit from the sewing machine. Despite their own patents on the invention, Wheeler and Wilson began paying their dues to Howe in 1854. This began an adversarial but amicable relationship that prompted Howe to come to Bridgeport to open his factory. Two years later, Howe and the Stockwell brothers created the Howe Machine Company in Bridgeport, certain competition for Wheeler and Wilson's business. However, the partners were secure in their own success. New York's *Daily Tribune* ran an article on their amazing factory, focusing on the modernity and efficiency of this "wonder."

The onset of the Civil War would make the sewing machine more than just a wonderful labor saver. A need for hundreds of thousands of uniforms for the army impelled trainloads of sewing machines down the coast from Bridgeport to New York, securing forever the technology's status in American society. Scores of seamstresses, working for much higher pay than previously, stitched together the coats and pants of the Union. Howe himself served in the Civil War as a private in the Seventeenth Connecticut Volunteers, though he was fabulously rich at that point and could have paid for a "substitute." He outfitted his own regiment with uniforms courtesy of his sewing machine empire. He also donated many of the profits he received from the lawsuit royalties to the Union cause.

During the war, Howe, Wheeler and Wilson were joined in Bridgeport by young Henry Alonzo House, born in 1840 in Brooklyn. He had been taught at home by his father Ezekiel, an architect and builder. As a boy, he and his brother James had shown creative promise when they built a small paddle-wheeled boat to carry produce and ferry friends. Unable to serve in the war due to a crippled right hand, Henry perfected a machine that would automatically sew buttonholes. He tested it in New York, and when it proved successful, Henry moved to Bridgeport to manage its production for the Wheeler and Wilson factory.

As the war years ended, a train crash stained these successes. Called the "Housatonic Railroad Slaughter" by *Harper's Weekly*, the accident shocked an America already worn out by death and destruction. On August 14, 1865, a freight train broke down six miles from Bridgeport and a passenger train nearly rammed it. The conductor, H.L. Plumb, backed the train slowly

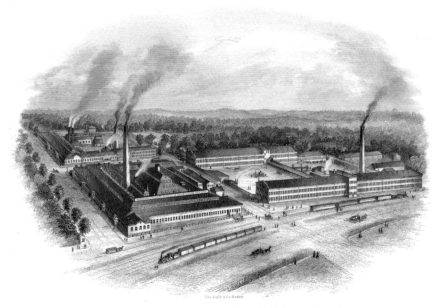

Before the Civil War, Wheeler and Wilson Manufacturing was the largest industry in town. *Courtesy of the Bridgeport Public Library Historical Collections.*

Tales from the Park City

away and walked to the rear of the train. As he reached the final car, he saw yet another engine hurtling up the tracks. After ringing the bell in a futile warning, he leaped to safety just as the engine plowed into the passenger train. The last car was nearly completely split in two. Plumb ran around to the front of the car, but the suffocating jets of steam from the ruined engine drove him out. Ten people died and twenty were seriously wounded or burned.

The mysterious third train turned out to be the Fairfield on its trial run. A complete lack of awareness on the part of the engineers had led the three trains out in succession, and carelessness with red flags resulted in tragedy. This was only one of the tragedies that would set back Bridgeport. There were several more train accidents in the following years, though none so serious. Despite this ominous setback, the second half of the nineteenth century was to be Bridgeport's golden age.

After the war, Elias Howe's machine won the gold medal at the Paris exhibition of 1867. Shortly thereafter, he died, exhausted from a life of work and conflict, lawsuits and war. Nathaniel Wheeler bought a house on Golden Hill and became immediately involved in philanthropy, serving on the board of education, the Bridgeport Scientific Society and the Fairfield County Historical Society. He was given the Knight's Cross of the Imperial Order of Francis Josef in Vienna and was made a chevalier of the Legion of Honor in France. Henry House went on to invent dozens of machines for a wide variety of purposes, including one that blocked felt hats, another that made paper bags and one that baked, handled and packed biscuits for the Shredded Wheat Company. A.B. Wilson retired twenty years after the war ended, secure in the knowledge that he had helped to forever transform the clothing industry. By this time there were ninety-six manufacturing companies in Bridgeport, employing thousands of workers. The destiny of the city was on track, and the seemingly simple sewing machine had taken it there.

Chapter 3

LINCOLN'S FIRST FRIED OYSTER

On March 10, 1860, Abraham Lincoln arrived in Bridgeport by train for his last campaign speech in New England. Arriving before noon, he spent the day at the house of Charles Frederick Wood on Washington Avenue, where his host treated him to his first plate of the local delicacy, fried oysters. The unusual but fortifying meal served the future president well that evening at a packed Washington Hall. The Greco–Roman Revival brownstone had been recently built in 1854, making it the largest venue in the city, but that night it overflowed into the streets. Men from the surrounding towns of Fairfield and Stratford joined Bridgeporters in the crowd, holding torches and cheering for this giant from Illinois. No one recorded his speech that night, but no doubt it was similar to the one he had been giving all over Connecticut. Filled with poetry and humor, his speeches made a strong appeal to end the institution of slavery and demanded, "As we understand our duty, so do it!"

After the speech, the presidential candidate walked to the Bridgeport railroad station and waited for the nine o'clock night express to New York. He had done his job and inspired the people of Bridgeport, who thronged around the tall figure to give him a rousing sendoff. He had moved their consciences and their hearts and changed conservative democrats like P.T. Barnum into abolitionists and "wide-awakes." Lincoln had mentioned Barnum in speeches before, and Barnum returned the favor by illuminating his mansion Lindencroft in honor of the presidential campaign. However, the showman may have noticed one conspicuous absence at Lincoln's speech: his friend William Henry Noble. Noble was the town's most prominent Democrat and would have perhaps felt out of place at a political rally for the new leader of the very "liberal" Republican Party.

Born in 1813, as a child William Henry Noble may have watched the great General Lafayette come through town. Graduating from Yale University with a law degree at age twenty-three, he came back to Bridgeport, was admitted into the bar and helped the city of Bridgeport secure its charter. He also taught French and Spanish in his father's school on Golden Hill. Noble's career blossomed when he became the secretary of Bridgeport Savings Bank in 1842, then the state's attorney in 1846. When his father died, he came into a huge inheritance of land in East Bridgeport and entered into an agreement with fellow citizen P.T. Barnum to develop it. Noble worked tirelessly developing this city within a city, assisting the construction of houses, hotels and factories. He planted trees on sidewalks and ensured space for parks. He also shared the cost of repairing the bridges to make this a viable and valuable part of the growing city.

Known to be generous and hospitable, Noble was a familiar figure in Bridgeport, often seen walking the streets. His wife, two sons and two daughters were favorites among their large circle of friends. Devoting what spare time he had to horticulture, Noble bred a unique species of pear, exhibiting it at expositions. In short, William Henry Noble had money, prestige and connections. He did not have to fight. But he would, and he would become one of many Bridgeporters to serve the Union in the most critical war America has ever known.

On April 14, 1861, Fort Sumter fell, beginning the War Between the States. With astonishing speed, four short days after the loss of Sumter, a train of Massachusetts troops crossed the Pequonnock River. Huge crowds at the Bridgeport depot welcomed and saluted them. On April 20, Mayor Sterling presided over a great "war meeting" at city hall. "The Star Spangled Banner" rang out into the rafters, speeches were made in support of Lincoln and the Union and money was raised for families of volunteers. Captain Richard Fitzgibbons and Captain John Spiedel were among the first Bridgeporters sent off on April 22. The Wheeler and Wilson Company band marched them proudly to the depot playing "Yankee Doodle." In all, Bridgeport men would fill seven companies by the fall of 1861.

Bridgeport's common council unanimously passed resolutions that included a statement of confidence in Lincoln and his cabinet and announced "that we extend to them our hearty sympathy in the ordeal through which they are passing and that we pledge to them our united and earnest support." The town also vowed to gather its full quota of soldiers to the war and kept the promise, sending huge numbers of men to potential death. Sergeant Major John Curtis of the Connecticut Ninth was one of those men. He earned the Medal of Honor for a fight in Baton Rouge, Louisiana, on August 5, 1862, when he went alone to the enemy line and captured two prisoners, walking them all the way back to the

Bridgeport

Union headquarters at the point of his bayonet. Though many of those first regiments would not see the end of five Aprils, Curtis survived, living until World War I.

Of course, not everyone in Bridgeport supported the war. Many companies did business in the South and were not pleased with the Civil War's effect on their profits. Unlike William Noble, some in the conservative Democratic Party had sympathies with the Southern states. On August 24, 1861, ten miles north of Bridgeport in the town of Stepney, a few hundred "Peace Democrats" who were urging reconciliation with the South held a "peace meeting." However, they were swarmed by a crowd of one thousand Union supporters from Bridgeport, many of whom were veterans of the disastrous Battle of Bull Run, scheduled to have a "picnic" that very day.

Elias Howe and P.T. Barnum joined the throng and quickly took the situation in hand. Barnum condemned the "peace meetings" as covers for secessionist sympathies. "In the present crisis, there are but two parties: loyalists and traitors. There are those who either sustain the Union, the constitution, and the National Government—and those who do not." These strong words showed how high emotions ran, even in the heart of the North. However, Barnum finished the speech with patriotism and humor, ending the counter-demonstration peacefully.

Later that day when the troops returned to Bridgeport, they were joined by thousands of others in a patriotic celebration. Unfortunately, the crowd turned ugly and focused its wrath on the offices of the *Bridgeport Daily Advertiser and Weekly Farmer*, which had controversially announced after the fall of Fort Sumter: "The truth is that it is the South that is resisting rebellion: one initiated by the Abolitionists and Republicans of the North!" The newspaper paid for this statement those few months later when the survivors of Bull Run smashed the press equipment onto the street.

Barnum and Howe both condemned this act as "mob violence," their own actions putting them far beyond reproach with other Unionists. Barnum's resolve for the Union encouraged him to turn his American Museum in New York into a showcase for the ongoing Civil War. It survived an arson attack from Confederate sympathizers, and soldiers were posted day and night at Lindencroft in Bridgeport. Though a Democrat, his friend William Henry Noble also saw the necessity of preserving the Union and turned against those in his political party who sympathized with the Southern rebellion. He wanted to serve the cause of Lincoln because it was "the cause of the Union."

Too small to fight, Bridgeport entertainers Charles Stratton and Lavinia Warren contributed their own bit to the war effort, entertaining a frightened populace. Mary Todd Lincoln had sent the newlyweds a set of Chinese fire

Tales from the Park City

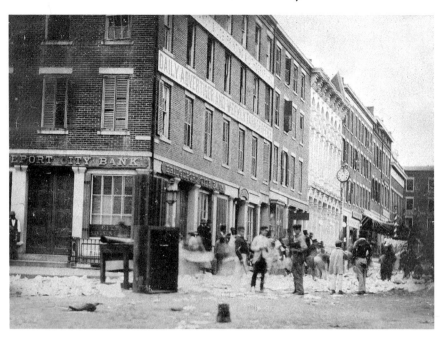

Aftermath of the August 24, 1861 riot in which veterans of Bull Run and other Bridgeporters destroyed the offices of the *Weekly Farmer*. *Courtesy of the Bridgeport Public Library Historical Collections.*

screens as a wedding present, and when they honeymooned in Washington, D.C., they received an invitation to be guests of honor at the White House. All of Washington's elite turned up for the reception. Lincoln himself bent his tall form down to gingerly shake their small hands with his enormous palm. Author Grace Greenwood commented on the president's sense of the "incongruity" of the meeting, and his famously dark humor obviously appreciated the droll entertainment during a bitter war.

Bad news in 1862 only encouraged the town. When Lincoln called for "three hundred thousand more," Bridgeport answered again. As William Noble said, "The soul of the North, unflinching before disheartening reverses, aroused to mightier effort." On July 19 at another war meeting in Washington Hall, Governor Buckingham joined Mayor Sterling to encourage the citizens and raise money. Elias Howe took the initiative, speaking to the crowd and enlisting himself. Both this selfless act and his continuing generosity throughout the war inspired hundreds of enlistments. One of these men was forty-five-year-old Dwight Morris, who had been a probate judge for the District of Bridgeport and member of the Connecticut General Assembly. Morris was appointed colonel of the

Bridgeport

Fourteenth Infantry, known as the "Nutmeg Regiment," and later would take charge of the entire brigade.

Another man swayed by these words and the cause of the Union was William Hincks, or "The Major," as his Bridgeport neighbors later called him. He enlisted as an infantryman to shore up the Fourteenth Connecticut Infantry and, with no boot camp, found himself in the thickest fighting of the war. In the cornfields of Antietam, Hincks survived a salvo of cannon fire in the disaster of "Bloody Lane." He described lying on the ground and being bombarded: "It was very trying to have to lie inactive under fire and listen to the hideous howling of the shell varied only by their crash in exploding and occasionally the shriek of some one who was struck. I lay closer to the ground than ever before in my life…and I never prayed more fervently for darkness than then." At Fredericksburg he nearly starved, writing in his diary how "hungry and cold" he was. He would be one of the few original members of the fabled Fourteenth to survive the Civil War.

Meanwhile, the army commissioned William Noble as colonel of the Seventeenth Regiment of Connecticut Volunteers. With one thousand men in the regiment under his command, he noted, "It was from the start known as the Fairfield County Regiment. With few exceptions, its ranks were filled by her sons." As a private in Noble's regiment, the fabulously wealthy Elias Howe always respected the chain of command. In addition, his sewing machine factory made sure that the Seventeenth was never without fresh uniforms. Colonel Noble mustered the regiment in the coastal farmland of Bridgeport on August 28 and eight days later left for Washington.

At the Battle of Chancellorsville, Stonewall Jackson's forces attacked the Connecticut Seventeenth under Noble's command. Positioned at the extreme right of the Union line, in the garden of the Talley House along the Turnpike, the Seventeenth held the line as regiment after regiment of Union soldiers broke and fled. But, as Noble said, "The crushing force of Stonewall Jackson's attack was in such irresistible mass, with such steady and unabating fire, that the air seemed full of whizzing rifle-balls. Their advancing light artillery threw a storm of shells down the lines of retreat." As the Connecticut regiment regrouped, rallying around the flag, Noble fell, his horse killed from underneath him. A deadly Minié ball hit him in the arm and a fragment of shell smashed into his left knee. Only the clogging of an artery prevented him from bleeding to death. Dr. Hubbard, the regimental surgeon, said the arm could possibly be saved but sent the fallen warrior home to recuperate.

For thirty-four days Noble stewed at home, while his men marched to the Pennsylvania town of Gettysburg. Bridgeport seemed empty of men.

Tales from the Park City

Besides the numerous companies already sent, the Second Connecticut Light Battery had also recruited almost entirely from Bridgeport and three more companies from Bridgeport marched in the Twenty-third and Twenty-fourth Connecticut Volunteers. The draft had come to Bridgeport earlier in 1863 but was unsuccessful, as it was to be elsewhere in the North, and it made President Abraham Lincoln briefly unpopular. Wealthy individuals like P.T. Barnum bought "substitutes," and many of these poor immigrants and destitute men deserted in the late years of the war. Seemingly in charge of the town, the Ladies' Relief Society raised money for soldiers, prepared and sent hospital garments and supplies and sewed mittens and stockings. Fearing the coming battle would be the most important in the war, Noble abruptly left his convalescence in Bridgeport to meet his regiment already at Gettysburg. Outnumbered and outflanked, they had made an early retreat on July 1 but stood their ground on East Cemetery Hill against the "Louisiana Tigers" on July 2.

The Connecticut Fourteenth also made their stand at Gettysburg, in the very thickest of the fighting. On July 3, William Hincks was subjected to the Confederate cannonade that preceded "Pickett's Charge." He said that he "sweat so much I turned the ground into mud." Hincks and the remaining 165 soldiers of the Fourteenth endured along the stone wall of Cemetery Ridge and helped turn back the advancing men from Tennessee, who marched farther into the North than any other Southerners. Hincks likened the battle to hell: "There was a sulphurous canopy, and men's ears bled from the roar." Brutal hand-to-hand combat between the troops ended the fateful charge, one of the decisive moments of the Civil War.

That same day, William Hincks captured the enemy flag in a daring action with two other soldiers, one of whom was immediately shot. He outran the third soldier in a hail of bullets and grabbed the flag of the Fourteenth Tennessee Regiment, bringing it back to his camp to cheers. His citation for the Congressional Medal of Honor reads, "The devotion to duty shown by Sgt. Maj. Hincks gave encouragement to many of his comrades at a crucial moment of the battle." Nevertheless, medals and speeches would be far off. The bloody battle ended with Hincks and the remainder of the Fourteenth Connecticut burying the countless dead.

Meanwhile, William Henry Noble arrived from Connecticut, not yet fully healed but ready to fight. He found himself in charge of the brigade and rallied what few troops remained. The regiment had been sparring with the Confederates on the edge of town and "it was very evident, on the morning of the 4th, that the enemy were in full retreat." Encouraged, Noble marched into the town of Gettysburg at the head of his beloved Seventeenth on

Bridgeport

Independence Day. They had lost 206 men during the three-day battle, but shipped out to South Carolina and then Jacksonville, Florida. Here Noble assumed command of the Second Brigade, and the Seventeenth moved to St. Augustine to conduct foraging raids.

On Christmas Eve 1864, Confederate troops captured Colonel Noble near the St. John's River in Florida. Later, he said, "The attack was sudden and unexpected. They are easily made so in Florida, which is pretty much all one pine wood." The soldiers took him to the infamous Andersonville Prison Camp, where he became the highest ranking imprisoned officer. In later years he often refused to speak of the horrors of this "snakepit." He and other prisoners attempted to tunnel out of the camp, but his captors released him in an officer exchange. Unfortunately, many of the Seventeenth stayed behind, forced to repair Florida railroads until July.

The few remaining soldiers of the Connecticut Fourteenth were present at the surrender of General Robert E. Lee's army on April 9, 1865. The next day Bridgeport sponsored a grand celebration to honor the end of the war. However, five days later, black flags replaced the tricolor banners when news arrived that President Lincoln had been assassinated by John Wilkes Booth. Obsequies were held in Bridgeport on April 19 and attended by thousands. Dr. George Loring Porter of Bridgeport happened to be the only commissioned officer present during the disposal of Booth's body, took charge of the medical needs of the other conspirators and later witnessed their hangings.

The Connecticut Fourteenth had been decimated from Antietam to Appomattox, and after participating in the grand review in Washington, on June 10 the few Bridgeporters like William Hincks returned quietly to their hometown. The D, G and K companies of the Seventeenth returned on August 4 to a more splendid reception. Elias Howe had survived the war as a private and purchased a special train for the men's transport. Talk that day centered on the empty seats of fallen comrades, but the reception at Bridgeport Depot was warm and friendly, reminding the battered soldiers what they had been fighting for.

After the war, General Ulysses S. Grant recommended that William Noble be brevetted brigadier general in the Union army. However, that would be the end of Noble's short military career. As he said: "When the cruel war was over the soldiery and officers had no other thought or longing, but for home, and to renew their toil of life." He returned to a law career in Bridgeport and helped veterans and their descendants acquire their pensions from the federal government. His interest in horticulture also led him to be chairman of the Board of Parks Commissioners. Later, Noble became a member of the

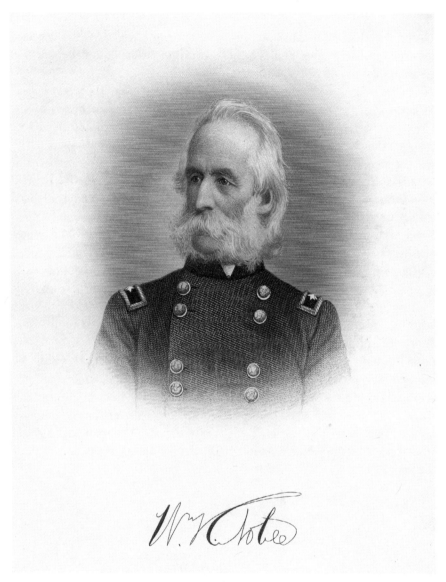

Later brevetted a general, William Henry Noble commanded the Connecticut Seventeenth Volunteers. *Courtesy of the Bridgeport Public Library Historical Collections.*

city council, senior warden of Christ Church and a state representative. He bought an old 1795 homestead on Stratford Avenue, where he could climb the captain's walk and watch the sea. William Hincks lived nearby in a house at Park Avenue and Prospect Street, marrying and bringing up three sons. He became a bank executive and helped P.T. Barnum found the Bridgeport

BRIDGEPORT

Hospital and Barnum Museum. His commander, Dwight Morris, received an appointment to the United States Consul of France after the war and became the secretary of state of Connecticut in 1876.

On June 30, twenty-one years after the Battle of Gettysburg, an elderly William Henry Noble and many of his fellow surviving members of the Connecticut Seventeenth took a train to the small Pennsylvania town. Though they arrived late, some of the veterans walked out to Cemetery Hill to "get their bearings." The next morning the rest found spots by barns or boulders where they had been wounded or lost a comrade. Then they formed lines and marched to the field where the regiment had suffered its greatest losses during the battle. General Noble presided, telling the assembled men, "War lives on a terrible sacrifice of life, and waste of substance. Yet greater evils can befall a people than the sacrifice of either upon the tented field."

Reminding them that history had already passed judgment on the nearly legendary War Between the States, he continued, "All over our wondrous country blue-coat and gray-back own and swear by that flag which from both its sides looks upon a people wholly free. Let it be our bounded duty and work, to bind up the wounds and build up the waste of war." Causing not a few tears to be shed by battle-scarred veterans and onlookers alike, he finished by echoing Abraham Lincoln's famous address: "A nation can only ride and live on the stamina and broad foundation of the whole people. It was the common people of this land that made the nation, or saved it, and only they will keep it, living down the ages, the glory of humanity, the grand achievement of the world, a nation of the people and by the people and for the people."

Chapter 4

WITH HER EYES TO THE SEA

Black Rock Harbor stretched out from the mouths of Ash and Cedar Creeks, separating three peninsulas off the south side of Bridgeport. The small, deep harbor created a perfect trading port and shipbuilding area during the 1700s and into the early 1800s. At its mouth lay an island of nine and a half acres, just large enough for a small farm holding. A man named Benjamin Fayerweather settled it in 1713 and his descendant, Daniel, sold it to the federal government nearly a century later. They saw the island as the perfect spot to build a lighthouse along the shore of what is now Bridgeport. First constructed in 1808, the wooden, octagonal Black Rock Harbor Lighthouse stood forty feet tall. It used whale oil for its "spider" lamp that helped mariners navigate the sometimes treacherous Long Island Sound.

The first keeper of the island, John Maltbie, died suddenly after a short five-month stint. He was followed by Isaac Judson, who stayed on Fayerweather Island until 1817, before Stephen Moore took over with his twelve-year-old daughter, Catherine. Unfortunately, Stephen seriously injured himself and was literally unable to perform his duties. But giving up their government pay was simply not an option for the poor, motherless family, so Catherine accepted the burden. She had learned to trim the wicks and polish the lenses as a child and now pitched in with the heavier duties of a full-time keeper.

On September 3, 1821, only a few years into the Moores' service, a hurricane smashed into the island. Every ship and boat in the harbor was forced onshore, and the original Black Rock Lighthouse was flattened. It took two years to build a new one. Catherine said, "It was a dreadful thing to have happen, for this was then the only light on the Connecticut side of Long Island—the only light between New Haven and Eaton Neck, and was of course of inestimable value to mariners." Luckily, the next lighthouse was built to stand the test of time. It stood forty-one feet tall, constructed of coursed sandstone ashlar with rubble mortar, and braved all future storms.

Bridgeport

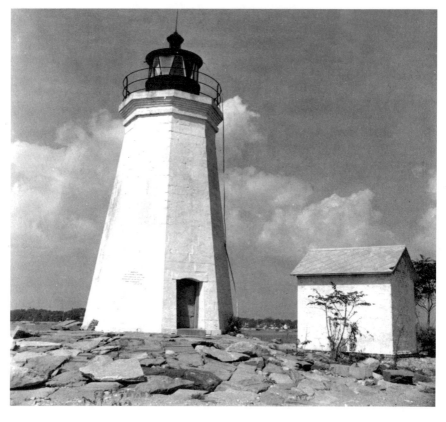

Black Rock Lighthouse on Fayerweather Island kept the harbor safe for over 120 years. *Courtesy of the Bridgeport Public Library Historical Collections.*

A cozy keeper's house and small oil shed huddled on the other side of the salt marsh, seven hundred feet away. The house proffered a modest kitchen, living room and one bedroom, barely large enough for the purposes of Catherine and her father.

Catherine, or "Kate" as she preferred, dressed in "boy's clothes" to do her duties. At night a lantern would swing from her bedstead and her hazel eyes would search the darkness, counting the number of boat lights. On rainy evenings, there could be as many as three or four wrecks, and she had to be alert. When it stormed, she had to hike over slippery rocks and planks, and often the wind was strong enough to knock her backward. The few hundred feet from the house to the light seemed like miles.

Kate grew her own food in a garden on the island, raised chickens and ducks and kept a flock of sheep that wandered around the nine acres and chewed the long grasses. She sheared them in summer to make her own wool clothing for the long, wet winters. She also took great care of the barrels that collected drinking water, since every attempt at a well ended in salt. "I never knew playmates," she said. "Mine were the chickens, ducks and lambs, and my two Newfoundland dogs." Kate may not have had a social life, but she did have purpose. No one else could keep Long Island Sound safe.

The "packet," or small sailboat, dominated the Sound in the early part of the century, speeding in and out of the harbors, growing faster and more efficient. These sloops increased in size to hold as much as seventy-five or one hundred tons of passengers, freight and mail, but they did not grow larger. This was actually a clever strategy on their part to avoid higher docking fees in other cities. As the century ripened, shipbuilding drew more and more investors, with farmers and merchants sponsoring this cheaper type of transport to Boston and New York. Big whalers began appearing at the city's docks, bringing in whale oil and ambergris for owners like the Bridgeport Whaling Company.

But the city's fishing fame would come from harvesting a much smaller sea animal. A huge natural oyster bed had been discovered centuries before off the coast of Bridgeport and Stratford. Now, a contingent of oyster boats mined the bed for "seed" oysters to "plant" in private underwater plots. The boats went deeper and farther into the Sound to reap barrels of bivalves that would be breaded and fried in hot fat. By the end of the century, thousands of bushels of high-quality mollusks were shipped to Europe, and the Bridgeport oyster industry consisted of nineteen steamships and two hundred smaller vessels.

Shipwrecks were common among all these classes of vessels. Kate personally saved at least twenty-one lives during her years at Fayerweather, dragging survivors out of the surf. Other sailors and swimmers also often washed up on the beach and Kate dragged them to her home for rest, tea and perhaps a plate of fried oysters. However, these were few compared to the number of dead bodies cleaned off the beaches of the island. "Hundreds," she claimed.

In 1830, an eight-lamp arrangement was installed for better visibility, but when the Sound was hazy or foggy, this was still insufficient to guide ships past the point or into the harbor. "It was a miserable one to keep going, too—nothing like those in use nowadays," Kate said of the system decades later. "It consisted of eight oil lamps which took four gallons of oil each night…During windy nights it was impossible to keep them burning at all, and I had to stay there all night." She did a good job. In 1850, an inspection team came by and gave her, or perhaps her father, high marks, pronouncing the job "first-rate." A fifth-order Fresnel lens was installed to improve her situation in 1854.

Bridgeport

Meanwhile, Black Rock Harbor's significance diminished in the region. A few miles to the east, Bridgeport Harbor was initially a bad place for navigation. A sandbar prevented larger ships from entering, and the wide, open mouth of the harbor was not as sheltered from storms as Black Rock or other nearby bays. That all changed when the city dredged a deep channel through the bar and built two long breakwaters arcing out into the Sound. These breakwaters needed their own lights but had to make do with a lantern hung on the end of a mast wedged into the rocks by Captain Abraham McNeil in 1844. Then a "decked-over" boat was used. Finally, McNeil drove a series of huge timbers into the mud to the bedrock and used to hang a lantern, creating what could barely be called a lighthouse. For twenty years, Captain McNeil and his son shuttled back and forth to the tiny lantern by rowboat whenever it needed to be fixed.

Surprisingly, this makeshift device did not trouble the next act in Bridgeport's evolution. The town transformed itself with the introduction of the machine that would change shipping forever: the steamboat. The first steamer to regularly shuttle between Bridgeport and New York was the *Fulton*, in 1815. It was a wonder of engineering at the time but not a very comfortable ride, with dangerous, dim kerosene lamps and freezing passenger compartments. The paddles made a terrifying roar for miles around, and a rudimentary sail could be used in case the newfangled contraption failed. In 1824, the route was taken over by the *General LaFayette*, possibly named in honor of his recent visit to the city. Other steamships docked at Bridgeport, like the *Nimrod*, the *Citizen* and the *Eureka*. In 1844, a ship called the *Mountaineer* made a new record for the New York to Bridgeport run at three hours and eight minutes.

This link to America's largest city increased the importance of Bridgeport, but there was little time for Kate to appreciate the change. Her life at Fayerweather Island bred constant work. The winters could be particularly hard and cold. Sometimes she could walk across the harbors on frozen surf, but the mainland could also be inaccessible, forcing her to butcher one of her beloved sheep. Even though Kate's work was doubled by taking care of her father, the invalid Stephen, she never complained. "I had done all this for so many years, and I knew no other life, so I was sort of fitted for it." In her spare time she planted ailanthus trees to stop the island's slow erosion. On nights when she had to watch the sea, she carved duck decoys out of driftwood with a knife.

It wasn't all merciless toil. At one point she brought two cows onto the island for the luxury of milk. For entertainment she assembled a library of over one hundred books. On the walls she hung the rules for lighthouse

Tales from the Park City

keepers side by side with original paintings, even an original Rubens. To make a little extra money, she tended her own private oyster beds. Occasionally, someone would row in from the mainland to poach her tasty mollusks. They were met by a shotgun and Kate's fierce words, "I represent the United States government and you've got to go."

In 1871, Kate's light was no longer alone on the shores of Bridgeport. Captain Abraham McNeil's son, John McNeil, returned from thirty-six years on the seas to become harbor master when the office was created. He had already been lobbying the city to do something about the Penfield reef, which was a dangerous area near the mouth of the harbor, and they decided to put him in charge. He finally built a real lighthouse in the middle of Bridgeport Harbor, a mile from shore. Standing on piles driven into the sand, the wood-frame dwelling was surrounded by an icebreaker and granite breakwater. The lamp-tower ascended from a mansard roof and a railed "porch" swung around the squat house, allowing keepers fresh air on calm days.

With illumination in place, the city continued improving the harbor, building a second breakwater so that the entire inner harbor could be dredged. Nathaniel Wheeler and P.T. Barnum were two of the owners who donated land for this purpose. This step is what truly advanced the Bridgeport Harbor far beyond Black Rock and ensured its prominence for merchants and fishermen. The Pequonnock River was also dredged, allowing yacht clubs to spring up farther back behind the commercial shipping areas. Steamers, canalboats and barges joined the old sailing vessels in the harbor.

Captain McNeil didn't stop there; he continued deepening and straightening the channel. The point of Stony Bar was chopped off completely and another channel was dug to the inner bar. McNeil was integral in getting a can buoy and storm signal system put in place for the first time. He also fixed Black Rock Harbor by dredging a deeper channel, removing built-up silt and building a breakwater. With no huge barges clogging up the bay, Black Rock was now set to become a yachting paradise, and enthusiasts immediately opened clubs, enjoying the shorter route to the waters of the Sound.

The last lighthouse to be added lit the inner Bridgeport Harbor from Tongue Point. The twenty-one-foot-high building was classically cone shaped but made from cast iron and painted black, without the brick lining used for similar lights. In 1885, a sixth-order classical lens was installed, replacing a lantern. A pioneering fog signal apparatus installed at the end of the century included a massive 160-pound fog bell that was struck by a clockwork mechanism run by heavy weights. Tongue Point Light's concrete and stone foundation originally poked hundreds of feet out into the harbor but was eventually moved back toward the western shore of the bay to facilitate easier shipping. The squat, black, beetle-like profile of this inner harbor light gave it the nickname "The Bug."

These improvements encouraged fierce competition from rival shipping interests. In 1879, the People's Steamboat Company's *Rosedale* began a route between New York and Bridgeport. The steamer sported plush red upholstery and carpeting, fancy brass fittings and sparkling, clean salons. Comfortable passengers enjoyed the smoking lounge and restaurant on their travels between the two cities. The entrenched Bridgeport Steamboat Company could barely keep up, and a battle for supremacy of the valuable route began. Bitter letters appeared in the Bridgeport newspapers and lies and rumors flew. Finally, an agreement was reached to divide the business, and in 1890 the Bridgeport Steamboat Company took over its rival and reigned supreme in steam.

By that time, things had changed radically for Catherine Moore. For fifty-two years, she had kept the lighthouse until her ancient father Stephen died. At last she was formally granted the title of "keeper," and the house, now expanded to eleven rooms, was officially hers. For seven more years, the fearless but aging woman kept the light and watched the Sound. Thousands of ships now passed by her every month, and many stopped in the now bustling Bridgeport Harbor.

Kate finally resigned her post in 1878. Her oyster beds allowed her to retire with $75,000 in the bank and she moved onto the mainland to a classy section of Black Rock, now officially part of Bridgeport. Her cottage stood near the Fayerweather Yacht Club, with a view of the lighthouse she had kept all those seasons. Once during those last years, she was asked whether she missed that home. She replied, "Never. The sea is a treacherous friend." Though she now walked along the beaches with a knotted walking staff, those who met her noted that her back was remarkably straight. Her features looked weathered and wrinkled, but her hair was still brown and her hazel eyes still bright with the sparkle of the sea.

Kate Moore's steely example may have inspired women like Mary Elizabeth Clark, the wife of the next keeper, who was a Civil War veteran and former whaling captain. When he died in 1906, she took over his duties briefly. After Captain John McNeil's brother, who ran the Tongue Point Lighthouse, died of old age, his wife Flora applied for the job. She was quoted as saying, "Although they were already giving up the idea of allowing women to become lighthouse keepers they knew that I had actually been the keeper of the light for twenty years and I was allowed to retain it without

Tales from the Park City

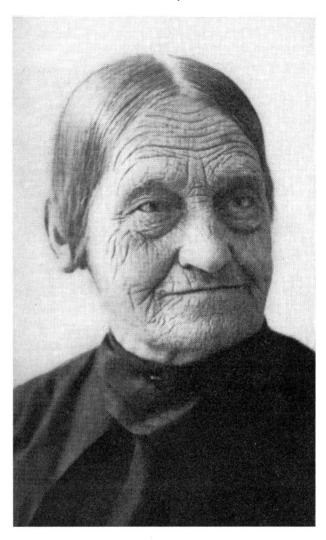

A weather-beaten but vibrant Catherine Moore in old age.
Courtesy of the Bridgeport Public Library Historical Collections.

even an examination." A remarkably progressive woman, Flora had shipped out with her father and learned navigation and the habits of sailors. She had also lived for some years in the strange sea-locked house of the Bridgeport Harbor Light with her husband, cheerily ignoring the occasional monster wave that crashed into her kitchen.

After her husband died, she lived on Lafayette Street and hurried between her manicure business and Tongue Point every day, wrapping a rubber coat around her classy business outfits. She fought the spray and bluster in all seasons and in huge storms, clambering out along the breakwater to tend the light or fog bell. Planks and rocks slipped under

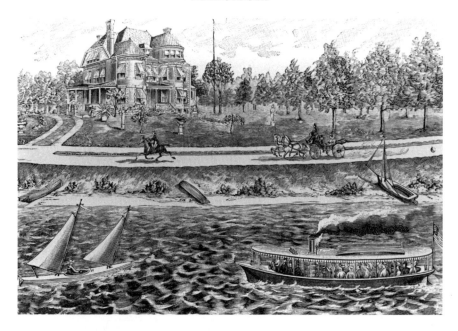

Seaside Park gave Bridgeporters a place to play on land and sea. Marina, Barnum's last home, was one of many shoreline mansions. *Courtesy of the University of Bridgeport Archives.*

her feet, water roared around her and wind tried vainly to push her into the gloom. Like Kate, Flora aspired to the full spectrum of life and, along with her two jobs, enjoyed paddling her canoe, playing violin or piano and painting beautiful seascapes.

These Bridgeport women were dynamic, creative and fearless pioneers. As Flora said, "I suppose some people would think it an impossible thing to do—and probably it would be impossible for them—but I am almost as much at home on or in the water as I am on land and I have no real fear of the water even when it is angry." Besides fighting the sea, Flora was a suffragette, and no doubt knew she owed a debt to women like Catherine Moore, who had proven long before that they were just as accomplished, if not more, as the ablest men. Flora retired the year her right to vote was enacted into law, another in a long series of strong women who stopped our fragile borders from eroding, saved drowning men and kept the lights lit brightly for the hope of future days.

Chapter 5

WHEN ANIMALS ROAMED THE STREETS

P.T. Barnum's broad nose, deep-set eyes, curly hair and receding hairline had become familiar to the people of Bridgeport by the latter half of the nineteenth century. With his signature cummerbund and bow tie, he appeared in the downtown shops with his red leather wallet, ready to buy gifts for his children or his wife. But it was not only trinkets that interested Barnum. Back in 1851, the showman had bought fifty acres from William H. Noble with the intention of building what he called "the nucleus of a new city." In what is now East Bridgeport, this land comprised a diamond-shaped peninsula separated from the main city by the Pequonnock River. Tree-lined streets were laid out and lots were sold to prospective homeowners and businesses. The carriage bridge became toll-free and a footbridge was added to increase pedestrian traffic to the area. With this act, Barnum had changed from show promoter to urban planner, and he had set his sights on Bridgeport.

During the Civil War, Barnum's passionate support for the Union triggered his decision to enter politics. In 1865, he was elected to the Connecticut legislature, though officially through the town of Fairfield. He voted for the Fourteenth Amendment and made a passionate speech decrying the use of the word "white" in the Connecticut constitution's section on suffrage. His speech was electric. "A human soul is not to be trifled with. It may inhabit the body of a Chinaman, a Turk, and Arab, or a Hotentot—it is still an immortal spirit!" In 1867, he was nominated for the United States Congress. However, despite the well-known corruption of his opponent, many newspapers outside Bridgeport slandered Barnum as a huckster and a cheat. He lost the election soundly.

Meanwhile, Barnum's famous American Museum in New York burned down. The fire roasted the animals alive, including whales that lived in a gigantic tank in the cellar. A varied and unique collection of oddities and relics

Bridgeport

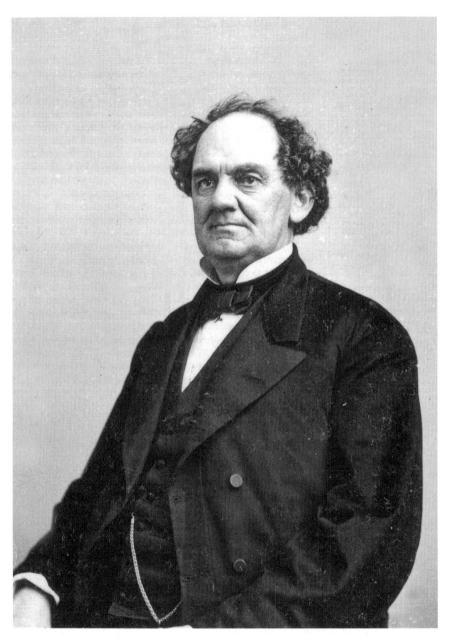

Photographer Matthew Brady captures P.T. Barnum at the height of his success, as probably the most famous man in the world. *Courtesy of the Barnum Museum, Bridgeport, CT.*

Tales from the Park City

valued at more than $400,000 disintegrated. Barnum rushed to New York from Bridgeport, surveyed the damage and initially considered retirement. Instead, he took the buildings of the old Chinese Museum, reopened and stocked the new building with new curiosities. Inspired by his enthusiasm, the people of both New York and Bridgeport continued to cheer him on.

Soon afterward, Barnum found taking care of his mansion Lindencroft simply too big a task for his ailing wife, Charity. He sold the sprawling manor with its statuary and topiary gardens and moved into another home near Long Island Sound. Famous city planner and architect Frederick Law Olmsted advised Barnum on the layout. He called it Waldemere, from the German phrase, "woods near the sea." Surrounded by a virtual forest of transplanted trees, it had a long pillared porch and a widow's walk from which to view the crashing Sound. There was a dressing room and bath for every guest room. He also built two cottages on the property, one for his daughter Caroline and the other as a guesthouse named the Petrel's Nest. His wife Charity finally found happiness at Waldemere, where she could smell the fresh sea air.

Whenever Barnum returned from his travels, a silk flag with the letters "P.T.B." flew gaily from the highest cupola. Mark Twain came down from Hartford and Horace Greeley came up from New York to visit, feasting with the Barnums on a shiny, gold-leafed dinner set. Though the showman had only ever been a moderate drinker, he became an abstainer, and there was no drinking with his guests. The visitors would relax on the sumptuous burl and curly maple furniture, their needs promptly served by a small cadre of servants. Barnum would lounge in one of his favorite seats, like the Texas Longhorn chair with arms and legs built from horns that supported a leather cushion. There he might open a volume of Whittier's poems and read them out loud, relishing the way the words fit to his practiced tongue.

Then the museum in New York caught fire yet again, and Barnum decided he didn't have the heart to build another. Turning away from the static arena of a gallery, Barnum seized on the purchase of a traveling circus. He promptly increased its size and magnificence and toured it around America. The characters and performers that had been put out of work by the ruin of the museum now had a new, nomadic life in the sideshow. Called Barnum's Traveling World's Fair, the spectacle performed throughout New England, Canada and the Midwest. Rhinoceroses, chariot races and lion tamers drew crowds, as did Barnum's integration of new automated machines and inventions. He shot a woman out of a cannon and helped popularize ventriloquism. He added "rings" to the circus, working up to the classic "three-ring circus" of today, which prompted excited visitors to come back for more shows. The *New York Herald* called him the "man of the future," who "feels it, sees it rushing up to us."

His first wife, Charity, died in November 1873 after many failing years. Traveling to Hamburg, Germany, to buy wild animals, Barnum could not attend the funeral. Instead, he retreated to London to spend some time alone. There his old friend John Fish and his daughter Nancy visited. Barnum fell for this kind woman, who was forty years his junior. Only ten months after Charity's death, he married Nancy Fish, but he declined to wear a wedding ring in deference to his previous marriage. Despite this inauspicious beginning, their matrimony was reasonably successful, and Nancy stayed with him until the end.

Despite managing the circus, Barnum remained a powerful influence in the growing city. He served as the director of the Pequonnock Bank, vice-president of the Bridgeport Board of Trade, moderator and trustee of the First Universalist Church and finally as mayor. In 1875, he was elected to the Republican ticket in a largely Democratic town. Bridgeport loved him, and it didn't matter his affiliation. He tried to improve the city's water supply, install gas streetlamps and support the entrance of African Americans into trade unions. But Barnum's reforming ways made him many enemies when he enforced the mostly ignored liquor laws, shut down houses of prostitution and investigated corruption within the city's government. Ousted after his one-year term, he remained on excellent terms with both friends and enemies, telling them, "In my efforts to be faithful to duty, I have never felt the slightest personal animosity, and I entertain for each and every member of this Council sincere wishes for their happiness and all the public approval which their actions merit."

The city now had a population of twenty-five thousand people. Growing rapidly, large sections now had the flavor of genteel suburbs, and huge Victorian and Gothic houses lined wide, elm-lined avenues. Streets in East Bridgeport bore the names of members of the Barnum and Noble families, and lots were set aside for parks and churches. As headquarters for Barnum's new circus, Bridgeport was perhaps more colorful than other booming industrial towns across the nation. Wandering downtown for a Sunday stroll, the townsfolk would often spot "giants," "dwarfs" or "bearded ladies" out for strolls of their own.

This colorful section of town was about to become bigger and more important with the first great merger of American circuses. Before joining with him, Cooper and Bailey's Great London Show competed against Barnum, promoting events such as the birth of the first elephant in America. "I had at last met showmen 'worthy of my steel'!" Barnum wrote. Instead

Tales from the Park City

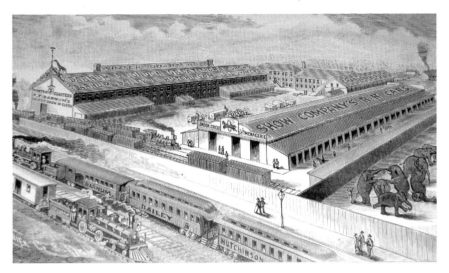

For fifty years, Bridgeport housed the Winter Quarters of Barnum and Bailey Circus. From train windows, passengers could spot performing elephants. *Courtesy of the Barnum Museum, Bridgeport, CT.*

of fighting with these rivals, he decided to join them in a "great alliance." The new super-circus would be called P.T. Barnum's and Great London Combined, then Barnum and London and finally, when a partnership with James Bailey was renegotiated, Barnum and Bailey Circus. By the late 1880s, Barnum dubbed it "the Greatest Show on Earth," and the name stuck, becoming part of popular language and culture.

The most famous addition to the circus was no doubt Jumbo the Elephant. Already famous in Britain when Barnum purchased him, Jumbo had taken children on rides at the Royal Zoo in London for twenty years. A great storm of protest and huge sums of money were offered against the purchase, but the excitement was already building on the other side of the Atlantic. The queen of England begged the American showman to relent, but this publicity only made the deal better and better for Barnum. Songs, cartoons and poems were written commemorating the event. American children deserved him, too, Barnum said, ignoring the "grief" of the British masses. All of New York hailed the showman as a hero, met the boat at the dock and followed him eagerly to what is now Madison Square Garden. The $30,000 that Barnum laid out for the purchase and transport were made up easily in the first two weeks. An instant star, Jumbo appeared in advertisements for both the circus and local companies like Sterling Baking Powder and Willimantic Thread. Barnum had struck gold again.

Bridgeport

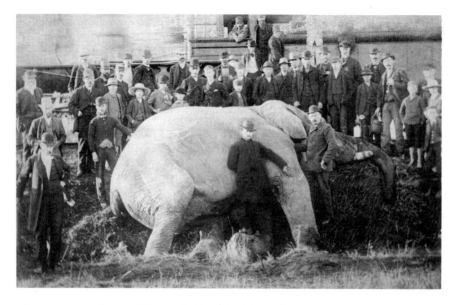

After success as a fixture of Barnum's circus, the beloved Jumbo died in 1885, after colliding with a train. *Courtesy of the Barnum Museum, Bridgeport, CT.*

Unfortunately, Jumbo's tenure at Bridgeport's Winter Quarters and celebrity in America was short-lived. While the circus loaded into cars on a fateful day in Ontario, an unscheduled express train barreled through the proceedings. The smallest elephant in the troupe, named Tom Thumb after Charles Stratton, was knocked down the embankment and broke his leg. Then Jumbo was hit, derailing the train and crushing his skull. It took 160 people to pull the huge elephant off the track. Barnum would try to replace the big attraction with other pachyderms like his "white elephant" and "Baby Bridgeport," but the American public never quite forgot the legend of Jumbo.

Charles Stratton himself often traveled with the circus as "Tom Thumb" to add celebrity to the proceedings. While on tour in 1878, his wife Lavinia's dwarf sister Minnie had died giving birth to a full-sized baby. Then a Milwaukee hotel fire nearly killed Charles and Lavinia a few years later. Their manager, Sylvester Bleeker, saved their lives, but his own wife desperately jumped from a high window and died. Six months later, while Lavinia was off touring, Charles died of a stroke at age forty-six. Working in Montreal, Barnum rushed home to attend the epic funeral with ten thousand others, and Charles was interred at Mountain Grove Cemetery. This amazing man had appeared in front of more spectators than any other performer of the nineteenth century.

Tales from the Park City

With Barnum's finances becoming increasingly complex rather than simpler as he aged, the showman offered the job of accountant to fellow Bridgeporter Henry Eugene Bowser in 1880. Bowser quickly discovered that he had a small empire to monitor. He issued monthly financial reports and pleased Barnum with his efficiency and verve. To assist him, Bowser hired another local named Charles R. Brothwell. Their office at 269 Main Street flurried with activity. Barnum's real estate holding alone was staggering, focusing on the huge developments of East Bridgeport. Barnum said, "That piece of property, which, but eight years before, had been farmland, with scarcely six houses upon the whole tract, was now a beautiful new city, teeming with life, and looking as neat as a new pin."

In 1883 alone, Barnum built thirty-eight single houses, twenty-eight double ones and sold lots for eighty-eight others. He laid sewer pipes, water mains and over 58,000 square feet of concrete for sidewalk. Black Rock Avenue and Barnum Boulevard were filled in and graded. Barnum had also superintended the construction of a three-story brick building measuring 95 feet along Main Street and an astonishing 206 feet in depth. This "recreation hall" for the public contained a large meeting space, gymnasium, skating rink, bicycle track, bowling alley, restaurant, dance hall and even a shooting gallery.

Due to these huge landholdings, Barnum paid more property taxes than anyone in Bridgeport except for the Wheeler and Wilson Company. Nevertheless, he spent a good portion of his money on philanthropy, most of it directed at his beloved hometown. When George F. Lewis, a doctor and Civil War veteran, came home to Bridgeport, he found the medical care completely absurd. The city had no place for very sick patients, forcing doctors to set up beds in the musty police department basement. Lewis proposed a hospital for the growing town, and Barnum was one of the many to jump at the idea. He contributed $5,000 to establish the new Bridgeport Hospital, which opened in 1884. Serving as its president, Barnum oversaw its infancy as carefully as a proud father.

When the two sloops that ferried passengers across Long Island Sound to Port Jefferson became insufficient for the demand, a man named Captain Charles Tooker approached Barnum and other Bridgeport worthies. After much discussion, the Bridgeport and Port Jefferson Steamboat Company was formed. Elected as its first president, Barnum, along with Captain Tooker, set about chartering the *Nonowantuc* to ferry across farmers, merchants and tourists. As the first official member of the Bridgeport Public Library in 1882, Barnum contributed hundreds of volumes to an institution vital to an educated public and proudly displayed his library card to friends and colleagues.

Bridgeport

Barnum popped through the door of his offices at 269 Main Street at all hours when home from trips to New York. Although either Bowser or Brothwell could have bilked the showman out of any amount of money without him noticing, they remained honest until the end. During the 1880s, Bowser often visited the Winter Quarters of the circus, by now one of the largest animal-training facilities in the world. It included 150 permanent employees, a dozen workshops and a 350-foot-long Railroad Building, in which one hundred circus cars and wagons were parked. Eight rail tracks connected directly to the commercial lines. In fact, the enormous complex needed its own steam-power plant.

Elephants played and trumpeted in wide, enclosed yards. Wild birds flew from roof to roof. Harness shops, costume tents and sawdust rings teemed with monkeys, lions, camels and giraffes. The stable alone accommodated several hundred horses. Trainers used the regulation-sized ring to work on the animal acts. In warm weather, the elephants would be led along Park Avenue south to bathe in the Sound at Seaside Park. Many human performers chose Bridgeport as their permanent home as well, and a decent portion of the town's small businesses served the circus's needs. Children of Bridgeport families lived in a constant wonderland of excitement, and gangs of kids stood outside the fences every day, hoping for glimpses of a zebra or rhinoceros.

Passengers on the New York, New Haven and Hartford train line could never quite prepare for the brightly painted buildings topped with flapping flags and surrounded by beautifully gilded and appointed parade wagons. An elephant hitched up to a plow often could be spotted from the train windows, providing a dramatic effect that created fascinated fans by the hundred. Occasionally an animal escaped and the citizens had a day of excited terror while the police and circus trainers searched the alleyways and parks.

On November 20, 1887, Barnum experienced his fifth and final fire, this time at the Winter Quarters of the circus. Only one lion and a few elephants survived, smashing through the wooden walls to safety. One elephant named Gracie leaped into Bridgeport Harbor and swam to Bridgeport's lighthouse before dying of burns. Like his countless museum fires, this tragedy devastated the showman. But he immediately built a new Winter Quarters on the smoldering earth, sure now in his newest and last great entertainment endeavor.

In 1888, Barnum built his last mansion, literally only a few feet east of Waldemere. He called it Marina, and it had the same excellent ocean view. He knew his young wife would need a modern place after he was gone, so he installed electric lighting and plumbing, which Waldemere lacked. They transferred the furniture and belongings out the door, across the grassy lawn

Tales from the Park City

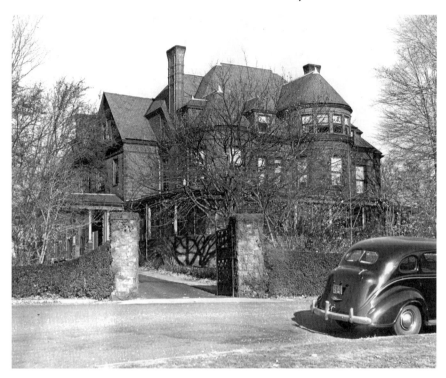

Built in 1888 for his young wife Nancy, Marina would be Barnum's last home, surviving into the twentieth century. *Courtesy of the University of Bridgeport Archives.*

and into the door of the new house. When they were finished, Barnum sold and hauled off two pieces of the old building and knocked down the rest, filling in the cellar and covering it with grass and trees.

Barnum had become close friends with both Presidents James Garfield, who called him the "Kris Kringle of America," and Ulysses S. Grant, who actually campaigned for Barnum in Connecticut. Shortly before Grant's death, Barnum visited him at his home, where the showman told the former Union hero, "General, since your journey around the world you are the best known man on the globe." "By no means," Grant laughed. "You beat me sky-high; for where ever I went—in China, Japan, the Indies, etc.—the constant inquiry was 'Do you know Barnum?' I think, Barnum you are the best known man in the world." The old general was probably right. Barnum's name had become synonymous with American capitalism, gumption and can-do spirit. He had used his boundless enthusiasm not only to entertain the world, but also to help transform his adopted town of Bridgeport into a thriving city.

BRIDGEPORT

In his last years he bought Shetland ponies and donkeys for his grandchildren to ride, and he would often perform tricks to amuse them. Once, at the local Boys' Club, he gave a talk that turned into a magic show. According to Reverend Lewis Fisher, his final pastor in Bridgeport, he put two hats on a table and told the boys that he would eat a biscuit, which then would appear under one of the two hats. They watched in rapt attention as Barnum asked them under which hat it should appear. When they told him, he calmly raised the hat, put it on his head and told the boys, "The cracker is under the hat."

At one point, Barnum briefly considered running for the United States presidency against Grover Cleveland. Instead, he continued to travel, but in 1890 he contracted a near-fatal illness and remained at Marina. A few days before his death, Barnum gave an interview for the *Newtown Bee*, telling the reporter that he wanted to be cremated rather than having people come in to gaze at his corpse and remark on his faults. With this, he told a story about a widower whose wife was cremated. The man affectionately preserved the ashes in a glass jar, but when he remarried, he used them on the ice on the front steps of his house, afraid his new bride might slip. With that morbid joke at the power of the future over our emotions, Barnum broke into a glorious laugh.

On April 7, 1891, at age eighty-two, P.T. Barnum died. A wreath of roses was hung on Marina's front door. The city of Bridgeport hung his portrait everywhere, and store owners and charities draped their buildings and windows in black. Flags across the city stood at half mast. On April 10, funeral services were held and Barnum was buried in Mountain Grove Cemetery in a brick vault under a two-ton slab across the way from Charles Stratton. The congregation sang "Auld Land Syne," crowding the wet streets under a gray sky.

After he died, his generosity to Bridgeport became even clearer. Along with various philanthropic donations to the Actor's Fund of America and the Universalist Church, he left $100,000 to build the Barnum Institute of Science and History, later known as the Barnum Museum. He had already endowed the museum of natural history at Tufts College in Massachusetts but wanted to leave one for the city he had come to love. The strangely Romanesque, nearly Byzantine building would give a home to the exhibits of the Bridgeport Scientific Society and the Fairfield County Historical Society and provide a lecture hall for speakers like Thomas Edison.

The city remembered him for this act and a thousand others, erecting an enormous statue by Thomas Ball that had been hidden in a warehouse in 1893. Many citizens chipped in for the enormous granite base in Seaside

Tales from the Park City

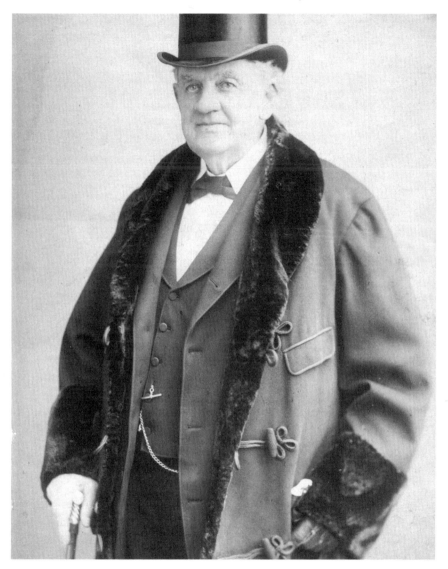

At the end of his life, P.T. Barnum turned to philanthropy, donating money and land to the city he loved. *Courtesy of the Barnum Museum, Bridgeport, CT.*

Park, on a spot that had been his favorite, in sight of his old home. However, they set his face not inward to the city he helped build, but out to sea, to the future. The year before he died, the showman wrote, "The noblest art is that of making others happy." Phineas T. Barnum had lived that art, and he brought happiness to his friends, the people of Bridgeport and the world.

Chapter 6

THE PLAYTHINGS OF POSSIBILITY

The first aroma to grace Joseph Frisbie's nose was no doubt fresh pie. When he was born upstairs from his parents' bakery on March 21, 1878, the day's order of pie was sliding piping hot from the oven. His mother, Marie Black Frisbie, had the midwife run downstairs to tell her husband William that he had a son. He was quite pleased but didn't stop his work getting the daily shipment ready. He had moved to Bridgeport a few years earlier from the Totoket area of Branford, Connecticut, where his family had lived since the exceptionally early year of 1620. His father had run a gristmill for the Olds Baking Company, so William knew baking, and he charged headlong into the family business. In 1871, at only nineteen years old, William bought an existing bakery at 147 Kossuth Street. He promptly renamed it the Frisbie Pie Company and began selling three hundred pies a day.

Joseph often mentioned his "pious" upbringing over the bakery to friends and associates, and the joke never got old. Living on the second floor of the building over a bakery made a deep impression on the young boy. His family business ran smoothly and regularly, with his aunt, Miss Susan Frisbie, supervising the pie making with an expert nose. His father William and family friend Charles Eckler delivered the fresh pies to the stores and residents of Bridgeport. They felt quite content with their small but successful business, even though all around them the city expanded like an enormous loaf of bread.

When the Frisbies moved to Bridgeport, the bustling manufacturing town had capitalized on its fame as the leading producer of sewing machines to tempt entrepreneurs. Dozens of small companies like Ives Manufacturing rose up in no time. Founded in 1868 on Water Street, Ives produced the first mechanical trains to run on tracks, as well as the odd cultural artifact called the Monkey Bank. Designed by hometown boy Charles F. Ritchel, the bank operated when a person placed a coin on the flat slide tray held by the monkey and then pressed a lever on its back. The arms rose up, lifted the coin tray and smoothly slid the currency through a slot on the monkey's stomach.

Founded on Crescent and East Main Street in 1865, the much larger Bridgeport Brass Company originally made clock movement pieces and brass frames for hoop skirts. As the factory expanded, it began to find various ways to shape the malleable alloy, producing tubing and sheets and parts for kerosene oil burners and lamps. It made bicycle lamps for this new and popular method of transportation, which became a rage in Bridgeport. Bicycle clubs, races and parades developed out of this enthusiasm, with hundreds of men and women participating. The parts for their bicycles were often hometown products.

When the electrical revolution swept America, Bridgeport Brass produced insulated copper wire, and the first telephone lines from Boston to New York were strung with its wire. Refrigeration wire, trolley parts, plumbing and tire valves were all part of the new cultural necessities that depended on Bridgeport Brass for their operation. With nearly one thousand employees and more patents than any other brass company in the world, it became one of the most successful industries to ever plant a foot in the Park City.

In 1866, two other manufacturing companies joined and moved into Bridgeport, taking the name of Union Metallic Cartridge and Cap Company. Metallic ammunition production began in earnest two years later, and soon the company contracted for solid brass cartridges and firearm components with the various countries of Europe. It built its own electrical generators, continued to expand and eventually would transform into the fabled Remington Arms ammunition plant.

Young Joseph Frisbie visited all the factories in Bridgeport in his spare time, learning the value of hard work. But he couldn't have had a better model than his family. When the blizzard of 1888 hit Bridgeport, monstrous fourteen-foot drifts stopped work for days. But the daunting blizzard did not stop pie delivery. Two days after the storm, Charles Eckler and William Frisbie hiked through the snow because drifts were too high and treacherous for the horse and wagon. Susan also kept their bakery sparkling clean, avoiding the pitfalls of so many failed fooderies. As Joseph said many years later, "Cleanliness has always been a paramount issue in our plant and our methods and care of preparation of the material we use is unequaled by the most fastidious housewife." Their clients showed appreciation and always welcomed William and Charles throughout the town.

Bridgeport

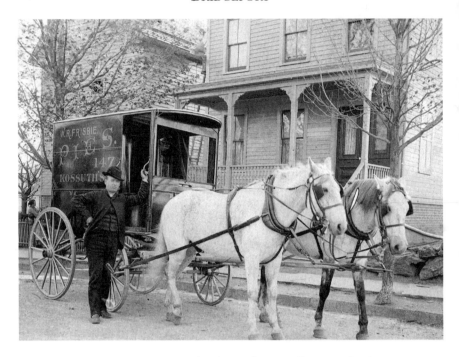

The Frisbie family knew customer service: for nearly twenty-five years, the pie wagon delivered twenty-seven varieties of fresh pastry to Bridgeport. *Courtesy of the Bridgeport Public Library Historical Collections.*

Most of Frisbie's clients shopped for the bulk of their merchandise at Read's Department Store on Broad and John Street, started way back in 1856. At one point D.M. Read's flagship store was New England's largest department retailer, with over 100,000 square feet on five floors. Farmers from the outlying villages might go to Wheeler and Howes for coal, fertilizer, animal feed or building materials. Real estate developers browsed the seven acres of wood at W.F. Swords Lumber Company. A Bridgeporter could go to the Franklin Typewriter Exchange for the latest in this fascinating technology or to Torrey and Hubert's if she wanted an oil painting for the walls of her stately home. Of course, for those who weren't fans of oil paintings, the two hundred retail shops that sold liquor and beer provided ample resource.

However, Joseph was not as interested in the sales end of the family business; what he loved was the hum and whirr of machinery. According to him, he was not a strong student in school but "had the good fortune of visiting rolling mills, foundries, brickyards." As a teenager he was busy learning how industry worked, as it leapt up around him faster than he could keep track. The Wilmot and Hobbs Manufacturing Company mastered steel and produced it in a seemingly infinite variety of forms, like stove rings, billets and lamps. It also made sheet and strip steel for sewing machines, bicycles, typewriters, bells and guns, some of them fashioned right in Bridgeport itself. The Jenkins Brothers company on Main Street began making six hundred kinds of valves in 1872. The Bridgeport Chain Company created chains for plumbing and sashes beginning in 1887. In 1891, the Salts Textile Works became the largest of its kind in the country. Breweries like A. Wintter and Company and the Eckhart Brothers promoted the bubbly lager beer that gained popularity in the later nineteenth century. The Bridgeport Crucible Company pumped out bicycle chain lubricant, graphite and of course crucibles. The new invention produced by the American Graphophone Company changed the entertainment industry with its "captured sound." The Canfield Rubber Company fabricated a rubber "dress shield," something that hardly seemed to justify its own factory. But Canfield molded five million pairs annually and shipped them around the world. Baked crackers, horse carts, watches, underwear...there seemed to be no limit to what the factories of Bridgeport could produce.

Living in this apple cinnamon swirl of ambition had made the young Joseph Frisbie more of a dreamer than his father, and he plotted to expand the small family business. He may have been inspired by three of Bridgeport's largest industries, which happened to be in three wildly different areas. The first of these to open in Bridgeport was the Warner Brothers Company, an enterprise that made that constrictive staple of nineteenth-century fashion: corsets.

Lucien and Ira DeVer Warner had been born in upstate New York, but when it came time to mass produce their improved, "healthy" corset for women, they chose Bridgeport. In 1876, at their factory on Atlantic and Lafayette Streets, they began production of these revolutionary garments, which used shoulder straps to distribute the weight and save women's spines. Ira's wife and hundreds of other women praised the comfort of the device, and soon these corsets traveled all over the world. Warner Brothers competed with the University of Corsets factory on Barnum and Ridgefield Avenues, a building that later became the Columbia Phonograph Company. However, the competition was slight, and the Warners dominated the industry. Their factory employed huge numbers of immigrant women, and to help them acclimatize to American society, Warner Brothers opened the benevolent Seaside Institute in a ceremony featuring the nation's first lady, Frances Cleveland.

Another entrepreneur who decided on Bridgeport as the best place for his factory was Waldo Calvin Bryant. The Bryant Electric Company started in 1888 manufacturing electrical switching devices, even though the first generating stations had only been created six years earlier. The primitive wiring at the time lay exposed on the walls and actually used wood as an insulator. Bryant invented the first "push-pull" switch, which decreased the size, cost and danger of the old switches. Originally, a mere eight employees built these new switches by hand, but as demand grew, the factory moved to an enormous 550,000-square-foot plant on State Street. It added lamp switches, plugs and various other wiring devices. Bryant was also a pioneer in standardizing plug design for electrical appliances. Forty years after it started, Bryant Electric took the title of the world's largest factory dedicated to wiring devices, producing four thousand distinct items.

Another important Bridgeport brand was the Holmes and Edwards Silver Company, built on mud flats by the railroad line between the old Mill Pond and Peacock Lane. Using a process called "extra sectional quality," Holmes and Edwards added protection to vulnerable parts of their forks, knives, spoons, ladles, tongs and servers. This allowed them to sell sterling at half the price of solid silver. Their use of the production line to fabricate silverware that seemed handmade increased their popularity. From 1882 to 1897, the Silver Company quadrupled in size to become the largest producer of table flatware in the entire world.

At the turn of the twentieth century, Bridgeport was shipping silverware, switches and corsets to all corners of the earth. From industries like these, Joseph Frisbie learned his most important lesson: mass production was the key to success. If these other commodities utilized assembly lines for their construction, why not pie? When William died in 1903, his son eagerly took over the family business. He promptly moved Frisbie Pies into a three-story factory down the street at 363 Kossuth and invented the world's first pie assembly line. To do so, he created a machine that spread the bottom pie crust. Joseph had seen a potter at work and applied the principle to making crusts. Built like a small potter's wheel, his fascinating "rimer," used for years later, was only the first of his innovations.

Flour that had been stored in the basement was sifted, mixed with lard and carried by automatic elevator upstairs. This dough went through a "crust roller" invented by Joseph and was then shaped on the "rimer." On the second floor, workers mixed and cooked fruit and cream fillings in big kettles. Sent through pipes to the ground floor, this mixture squirted into the crusts before going in the ovens. The company motto was "to follow along with the seasons," making various kinds of pies as the fruits ripened. Apples, blueberries, blackberries, cherries and huckleberries found their way into the pies at one time or another. Mincemeat, aged in kettles upstairs, was baked

Tales from the Park City

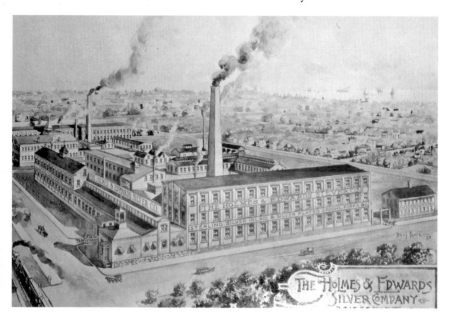

An 1893 lithograph of the Holmes and Edwards Silver Company's factory, the world's largest producer of table flatware. *Courtesy of the Barnum Museum, Bridgeport, CT.*

into crusts and delivered to patrons during the holidays. In all, four different sized pans held twenty-seven different pies.

Joseph also installed his own power plant in the basement of the factory, the first in his area of East Bridgeport. It was one of the last areas in town to be connected to the larger world, even though the rest of the city had long since begun its modernization. The Bridgeport Gas Light Company had long provided the community with gas for illuminating, heating and cooking, while the Citizens' Gas Company on the shores of Cedar Creek generated energy for the residents and manufacturers. Back in 1859, residents used tiny gas furnaces, irons and a few gas ovens. When the Frisbies first moved to town, gas began to be used to generate steam. Soon it was heating large ovens at bakeries. By 1895, the vast majority used it for home cooking on their new "gas stoves."

Electricity flashed into Bridgeport shortly afterward. Two franchises set up their dynamos and competed for the arc-lighting business of the city. Then the Bridgeport Steam Heating Company got into the act, as well. In 1884, the Connecticut General Assembly forced it to change its name to the Bridgeport Illuminating Company. In 1885, there were only fifteen arc lamps on the streets, but the electric companies soon put the old kerosene lamplighters out of business. The city signed its first streetlighting contract at fifty cents a lamp, and in a few years there were over one hundred lamps punctuating the dark streets. In 1889, the drawbridge at Stratford Avenue became the first bridge in the country to be equipped with an electric motor. During the dedication, showman P.T. Barnum walked a troop of circus elephants across it to demonstrate its effectiveness. The competing power franchises eventually combined to become Bridgeport Electric, joining with a company in New Haven until the great consolidation of Connecticut power companies into United Illuminating in 1899.

Bridgeport had already connected with the rest of Connecticut and the larger world in 1879, when Marjorie Gray became its first telephone operator. Then, in 1886, the Bridgeport-based Western Union Company gained control of a telegraph line from New York to Boston. In 1893, three companies combined to form the Bridgeport Traction Company and provide the large city with streetcars. They connected their lines to the New York, New Haven and Hartford Railway, which doubled in capacity during the last quarter of the nineteenth century and became the first rail in the country to implement electrification.

So by the time Frisbie modernized and expanded his business, Bridgeport was far more advanced than most cities of the time. And Joseph's self-powered, mass-producing "Pie Company" was an outgrowth of that revolution. As he liked to say, "Pie is a modern institution; the fact that pie was not invented earlier in the history of man is one of the contributing reasons why the pathway of life has not been as smooth as it might have been." Joseph had clearly hit on something, and the Frisbie business continued to thrive. In 1915, the horse and wagon used by William was replaced by a Ford truck, identical to the paddy wagon of the police, which now received the local nickname "pie wagon."

Joseph had learned another important lesson from his time in the Bridgeport factories: a good businessman needed to have uniform machinery to expand. To open plants in Hartford, Poughkeepsie and Providence, the bakery entrepreneur would take a hint from Harvey Hubbell. Hubbell's father had manufactured quality men's underwear, but Harvey saw the future of industry in mass production, perhaps inspired in turn by pioneers like the Bullard Machine Tool Company. Founded in 1880 and located in the Black Rock section of the city, Bullard built lathes, boring mills and turret machines to be used in hundreds of other businesses.

In 1888, Hubbell opened his own small business, which built machines and tools for other industries. He outgrew the building and had to buy Barnum's school building for his new factory, which eventually sported a giant electric sign shaped like a light bulb on the roof. Hubbell Tool and

Tales from the Park City

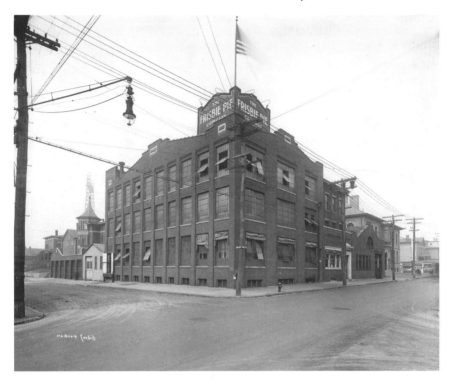

The Frisbie Pie Company's machines piped hot filling into waiting crusts on the floor below. Eventually the factory could produce eighty thousand pies a day. *Courtesy of the Bridgeport Public Library Historical Collections.*

Machine Works also made brass machine screws, wiring devices and pressed sheet metal for factory equipment. Along the way, Hubbell also invented the pull-chain electric light socket, the toggle switch and a number of other wiring devices. These devices developed into the industry standards, and Hubbell was known as the "Tiffany of the industry."

Bridgeport hit on this unusual new industry at exactly the right time, and by the twentieth century thousands of manufacturers around the world depended on Bridgeport's machines to craft tractors, vacuums, refrigerators, textile machinery, boat motors and elevator equipment. But neither Bullard, Hubbell nor anyone else made equipment for baking pies. So Joseph Frisbie decided to construct his own. He had already installed a machine shop in the basement to build the assembly line for his Bridgeport factory. Now he built more as his business expanded, requiring new factories and a fleet of trucks to supply 250 routes in New England and New York.

Bridgeport

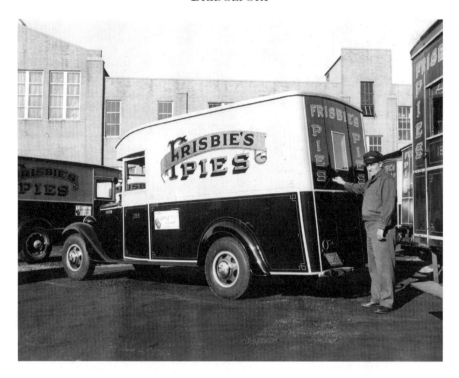

The fleet of Frisbie Pie Company trucks prepares for its daily run. *Courtesy of the Bridgeport Public Library Historical Collections.*

By this time, Frisbie was by no means the only famous bakery in Bridgeport. In 1898, Solderholm's Bakery opened on Maplewood Avenue and soon became known for its Swedish rye bread. It was one of thirty bakeries in Bridgeport at the turn of the century and eventually produced eighty-five thousand loaves a day. Borck and Stevens built their bakery on Tom Thumb Street in the former stable of Charles Stratton. They started making bread in 1915 and did well enough to later move out of the famous entertainer's stable into a big factory. In 1888, Frederick Bradbury had begun making the unfamiliar treats of crullers and doughnuts. By 1920, Bridgeport was the doughnut capital of the United States. Then Continental Baking bought out the Bridgeport Bread Company on Housatonic Avenue and Wells Street to bake Wonder Bread. Bridgeport ovens baked Italian bread, baguettes and challah for consumption or distribution, but none could compete with the company citizens lovingly referred to as "Ma Frisbie." Everyone remembered the days when their parents had stopped by the three-story bakery on the way home from the factory to buy a broken blueberry pie for a nickel.

Tales from the Park City

However, it would not be these tasty pies that made the family company a legend outside of Bridgeport. Frisbie's own pie pans were cut from large sheets of steel and hot-dipped in tin coating. When the pie was eaten, the tin revealed six small vent holes in the center in a star pattern. Both the ten-inch pie tin and later the sugar cookie tin lid could easily be made airborne and were unusually stable while in flight. The truck drivers began tossing the used tins on the loading docks during breaks, finding that not only were they easy to throw, but also that they hummed as they zipped through the air. When asked years later about the pie tins, an employee of the bakery from the 1920s confirmed, "The drivers tossed back and forth to each other demonstrating the various tricks that could be done with them." This play developed into competitions at the factory, and later Yale students from nearby New Haven picked up the game. They shouted "Frisbie!" to ready the catcher, who needed to be aware or risk having a tin disk slam into his head. The sport that developed was named "Frisbie-ing" by thousands of college students across the country. During World War II, those young men went off to fight fascism and the pie tin and cookie tin lids flew across the lawns of military bases across the world.

In the long run, the revolution started by Joseph Frisbie would lead to his downfall. Run out of business by the mass-produced frozen pies and pre-made crusts of the supermarket era, the bakery closed just one year after Wham-O tossed the "Pluto platter" onto toy store shelves. Shortly afterward it was forced to change the toy's name after everyone who had been playing the game for years called it what it was. Cleverly trademarked with one letter changed, "Frisbee" became one of the most popular games of all time, selling hundreds of millions to children and college students across the world. Perhaps it would not have been the legacy that Joseph or his family would have wanted, but in Bridgeport, intentions are often the playthings of possibility.

Chapter 7

BECOMING PARK CITY

For those traveling between New York and the cities of New England, the familiar sight of the Old Mill Green near the Pequonnock River marked their progress. Here the King's Highway swung north to avoid a long tidal estuary, splitting to create a long triangular lawn with ancient, shady trees. One massive elm ruled the Green, an elder tree that George Washington was said to have napped under on his stop here when traveling to Cambridge in 1775. But as the nineteenth century reached its midpoint, the green starburst of the Washington Elm was soon hemmed in by gray. Smokestacks competed with church spires for the skyline. Red brick overtook white clapboard as the dominant color. As early as 1857, Mayor Philo C. Calhoun said, "The want for such a place in our crowded limits for the free circulation of air and healthful exercise is seriously felt by our citizens, and universally remarked by visitors." And so it seems a singular miracle that as enormous factories began to crowd the landscape after the Civil War, Bridgeport did not become a wasteland. Instead, through foresight, planning and knowledge that the gray must be balanced by the green, a city born of industry and toil became known as the "Park City."

The origin of the name is not clear, but it may have come from *Morning News* reporter Arthur French in 1880, reacting to a spate of nicknames for other Connecticut cities. The first use of the phrase by the Park City Dye Works encouraged a slew of other companies to adopt the name. But when Mayor Calhoun called for the greening of Bridgeport, only one public park existed other than the Old Mill Green, a spackle of grass bordered by State, Broad and Bank Streets. However, William Noble and P.T. Barnum had thought ahead, preserving four acres of native forest trees in their East Bridgeport domains a few years before in 1851.

They recognized that a park in the center of their "New Pasture Lots" would make the rest of the housing more pleasing to the eye and the heart.

Tales from the Park City

Bordered by Barnum Avenue, Kossuth Street, East Washington Avenue and Noble Avenue, Washington Park was surrounded by fine homes and churches, making it a natural place for townsfolk to gather and relax. Converging walkways met at a bandstand in the center and the numerous leafy trees afforded the luxury of shade during hot summer days. In 1865, Noble and Barnum gave it as a gift to the city to become an official public park, the first of many.

The other "green space" in the city at the time was Mountain Grove Cemetery. Laid out in 1849, the cemetery integrated a beautiful park-like rural setting, away from the center of the city on the border of Fairfield. Built along the lines of many European cemeteries, castle-like gatehouses led into a labyrinth of pleasant walkways. Small emerald hills and shady trees surrounded calm, reflective ponds. Sparrows flitted through the elms and beeches, while egrets hunted for crayfish along the curves of Ash Creek. In this idyllic setting, the nineteenth-century habit of walking among the gravestones of the dead soon became popular in Bridgeport.

But the park that would cinch the city's contradictory title came about in a mix of chance and generosity. To the southwest of the public wharves in Bridgeport Harbor, a rocky piece of farmland remained completely unapproachable by horse or carriage. An oversight had failed to extend the roads down to the waves of Long Island Sound, and the shoreline remained strangely rural. The Seventeenth Connecticut Volunteer Regiment changed all that when it camped on these broad fields before shipping out to the Civil War. The camp drew attention and visitors to the area, and the rocky pastures, wooded patches and marshes became a topic of conversation in both drawing rooms and city hall.

The shoreline from Bridgeport Harbor to Black Rock Harbor was admittedly poor agricultural land, spattered with boulders and swampy sinkholes. Only one narrow path allowed access to locals who wanted to clam or bathe. No beach existed, and private landowners claimed the rocky promontory all for themselves. At the behest of the town's elders, P.T. Barnum and a handful of other public-spirited citizens wore down the farmers' resistance, leading to wealthy businessmen buying the land for the city. Tied up in legal proceedings, one farm could not be pieced out, so Barnum bought the whole thing and used the inland portion for his home of Waldemere. Land was also donated by Nathaniel Wheeler, John Brooks and George Bailey. This home of cows and cormorants was about to transform into the first "rural," marine open space in the United States, Seaside Park.

Wheeler solicited eminent architects and city planners Calvert Vaux and Frederick Law Olmsted to sketch a plan for the land. These worthy

BRIDGEPORT

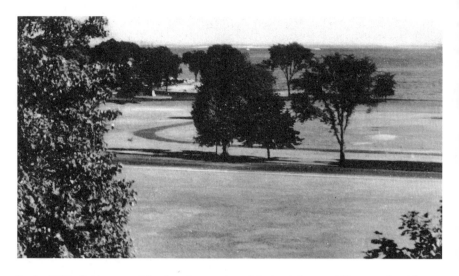

In the 1860s, Bridgeport philanthropists purchased the land that would become Seaside Park, the first "rural" marine park in the United States. *Courtesy of the University of Bridgeport Archives.*

designers, whose other designs included Prospect Park in Brooklyn and Manhattan's world-famous Central Park, presented the city with a drawing just after the Civil War. The architects said that "the leading feature of the site is undoubtedly the opportunity it offers, for the enjoyment of the sea breeze and an extensive view of Long Island Sound." A sea wall was erected, a drive and walk were plowed and a seawater pond called Mirror Lake was dug. Engineers drained and dyked a section between Park and Iranistan Avenues, creating the crux of the nineteenth-century landscape. As the decades passed, Barnum and other wealthy citizens contributed money to help drain and fill the area west of Iranistan Avenue, creating embankments and roadways and expanding Seaside Park west toward Black Rock Harbor. Circular drives and grassy lawns created more than a town beach: it was a center for municipal events, social gatherings and athletics.

Thousands of Bridgeporters enjoyed the park, shuttled there by the city's new horse-railroad system. The lively music of singers and orchestras thrummed from the bandstand. A colorful merry-go-round absorbed the city's children. The new sport of "base ball" was played on the broad lawns while fishermen cast their lines from the sea wall, pulling in bluefish and mackerel for their family meals. An oval track hosted trotters and sulky racing to the delight of gamblers and families alike. Visitors dressed in their finest dresses, hats and suits, carried colorful parasols or stripped down in the bathhouse to red-striped swimming trunks. They picnicked amongst the glades of cool trees, attended clambakes and sponsored bathing parties. Thomas Bender, in the *New York Intellect*, stated with prescient insight into Bridgeport's future populations, "The people in the park represented diverse, interclass, and interethnic democratic culture." He continued by giving Seaside the highest of praise: "There is no other park like it in the country, so near the city, with miles of walks and drives along the shore, where the waves break pleasantly in fine weather, or dash in might and magnificence when driven by the storm."

Meanwhile, the very shoreline of Bridgeport itself expanded beyond the central front of Seaside Park. To the west, between the Ash Creek tidal estuary and the headwaters of Cedar Creek, the peninsula of Black Rock thrust into the Sound like a great hand. Named for the high dark rocks at its tip, the fist of land had long been part of the town of Fairfield. However, Black Rock lacked a railroad stop or steamboat route and waned in power. As the neighborhood declined in prominence and Bridgeport prospered, some thought it best to throw their lot in with the industrial giant. The larger city generously embraced the colonial Fairfield neighborhood in 1870. With Black Rock Harbor now entirely within the city limits, the dual harbors gave Bridgeport even more influence over the Connecticut coast.

At the turn of the century, merchants and statesmen had already built enormous mansions and stylish Victorian cottages in Black Rock. Along the

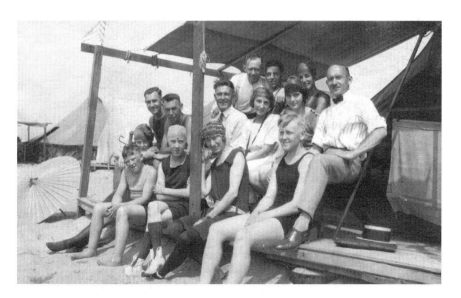

Beachgoers relax in the tent city built on Fayerweather Island about 1920. *Courtesy of Joseph E. Nechasek.*

shore at the tip of the peninsula an area called St. Mary's by the Sea was the most desirable, where large mansions with old trees and wide lawns provided a respite for the city's wealthy. A seaside walkway with a thin strip of planted trees gave residents of every social class a chance to stroll leisurely and watch great blue herons search the twin inlets for fish.

This green revolution did not pass by the northern reaches of Bridgeport. In 1878, a cattle baron named James Walker Beardsley donated a large tract of land by the Pequonnock River to the city. After seeing a group of city children kicked off a meadow by a nearby landowner, he decided they needed "a place that would always be theirs to play in." Six years later, famous architect Frederick Law Olmsted was hired again to landscape the river valley in the style of Seaside Park. He had more natural landscape to work with this time and took full advantage of the bucolic river and hills. Damming the river created Bunnell's Pond, which spilled over the weir in a pleasant waterfall. Colonies of ducks and geese immediately moved in. Local fishermen quickly found the pond a haven for largemouth bass, pickerel and yellow perch, while local children found it the perfect place for cooling off in the summer. Couples strayed across an inviting bridge to a small, wooded island. The pleasant rustle of the falls flowing over the dam and the chance to see a night heron made it a treasured, private spot.

Sculpted and landscaped, the small hills surrounding the pond exploded with shrubbery and flowers, oaks and birches. Purple-leafed European beeches were planted, their smooth, gray bark providing space for decades of lovers to carve secrets. Despite the charming stone bridges and terraces, it was never landscaped too heavily. Instead, the park's design looked and felt rural, with "rustic arrangements of boulder and parterre." In fact, it remained essentially rural in very important ways. Deer and foxes snuck into the park to feed, coming from the huge undeveloped tracts of forest to the east. This strangely untouched area straddled the border of Stratford and was home to raccoons, woodland turtles and wild turkeys. Eventually called Remington Woods due to its proximity to the gigantic factory, this land of meadows and wetlands provided a last home for the wild creatures driven out by development. A visitor to the new park could see this forest and beyond from the Beardsley Park terrace, the highest point in the city. Looking south across the whole sweep of Bridgeport, one could spot the sparkling indigo waters of the Sound.

The east side of the Park City changed radically on April 18, 1889. The borough of West Stratford was annexed, adding a substantial fraction of land and populace to East Bridgeport. Called Newfield, the addition included a long stretch of land on the other side of the Yellow Mill Pond and, across

Tales from the Park City

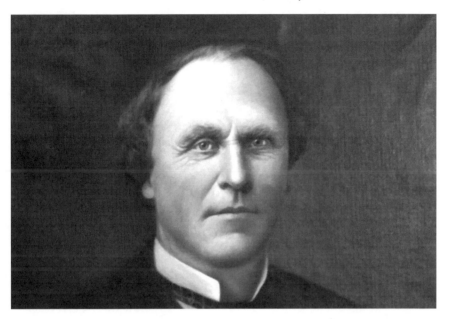

Cattle baron James Beardsley donated land that would become Beardsley Park in 1878. Painting by S. Elizabeth Nason, 1895. *Courtesy of the Barnum Museum, Bridgeport, CT.*

a salt marsh called Lewis Gut, a triangular island. The small, peninsular island, about thirty-seven acres, gave Bridgeport complete control of the harbor area, as well as new opportunity to increase its green spaces. Two liquor dealers, J.H. McMahon and P.W. Wren, decided to turn the island into an amusement park in 1892, playing off the legend that Captain Kidd had buried one of his treasures there.

These commons and parks soon housed sculptures and monuments that would make any city proud. A statue commemorating the achievements of Elias Howe was deemed too "lifelike" for Central Park and shipped to Seaside on the paltry condition that the city buy a base for it. The inventor's likeness stands leaning on his cane and holding a hat in his left hand. The townsfolk also remembered the millionaire's faithful service in the Civil War as a lowly private alongside his fellow Bridgeporters, and the Grand Army of the Republic post was named for him. The GAR raised its own monument, a "Pro-Patria" in Mountain Grove Cemetery. A Bridgeport sculptor named Paul Winters Morris fashioned it and gave it the form of a large bronze bas-relief mounted on a granite stele. The soldiers are pictured with heads bowed, and the legend states, "In Loving Memory of Those Who Did Not Return."

Morris was also tapped to build an enormous monument by the widow of William Hunt Perry, who happened to be his neighbor. However, he declined the honor, feeling the task too large for his talents. Instead, the memorial to the manager of the Wheeler and Wilson Company and parks commissioner passed to none other than Henry Bacon, the designer of the Lincoln Memorial in Washington. The Perry Arch towered at the entrance to Seaside Park, funneling traffic from Park Avenue under its triumphal twin arches. Bacon built it of Vermont granite, and his predilection for Greek themes was apparent in the Ionic pillars and portico. A plaque by Adolph Weinman near the base depicts Perry rakishly holding his hat and coat, while his wife Harriet carries a fruit basket.

The Ladies' Soldiers' Monument Association also erected a Civil War soldiers' monument in Seaside Park. Designed by William Moseman of Massachusetts in 1876, it was dedicated in a procession of military brass that ended in a sudden storm, forcing everyone indoors. In the dry opera house that night, speakers like Major William H. Mallory and General William Noble remembered the fallen of the Civil War in stories that moved even the hardest spectator. The Reverend Dr. Alexander R. Thompson spoke of the "millions of bondsmen set free" and of the soldiers by whose work "the land was saved." The elaborate fifty-four-foot granite monument reached for the sky in a stagger of bronze statuary, with an arched canopy leading up to a ten-foot bronze female figure representing the American Republic.

The enormous bronze of a seated P.T. Barnum staring out at his sea of possibilities would round out Seaside's sculpture. At the north end of the city, a statue was dedicated to James Beardsley. The cattle baron himself had been murdered a few years earlier, injured by burglars who had invaded his home. The thieves grabbed a good deal of his riches and were never caught. Even so, they could not take away what he had done for Bridgeport, and now his likeness stood proudly in bronze at the entrance of the park he donated. Finally, in 1912, a fountain dedicated to Nathaniel Wheeler was built at the intersection of Park and Fairfield Avenues. An emerging sculptor named Gutzon Borglum designed and built it, and upon completion he actually baptized his child in it. Mermaids and sea horses chase fish in this unusually expressionist piece, so unlike the sculptures that in later life he would become famous for. Borglum returned in 1923 to carve a figure of Christ for the altar of St. John's Church, a few years before beginning his masterpiece, Mount Rushmore.

These statues and memorials added a classical atmosphere to the city that may have gone unnoticed in the sweep of brick and concrete, if not for the legion of green spaces that flourished and prospered. Fairchild Memorial Park, Elton Rogers Park and Clinton Park all joined the throng. Spots like the gazebo of Wood Park became favorites among the locals. Svihra Park

Tales from the Park City

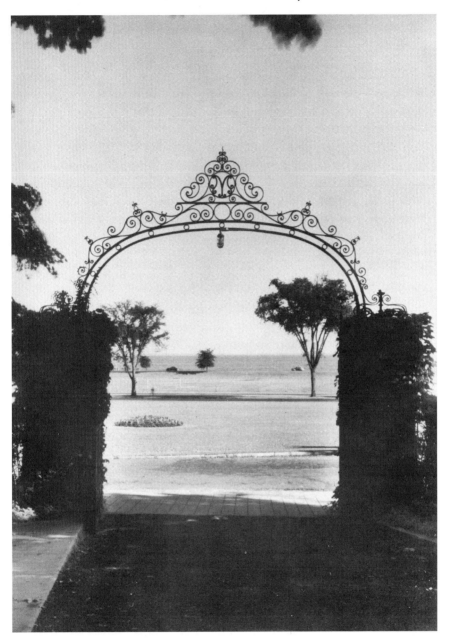

Through the gates of Marina mansion, Barnum's guests could stroll leisurely into Seaside Park. *Courtesy of the University of Bridgeport Archives.*

birthed another cemetery perfect for contemplative walking, while the misnamed Beechwood Park, which honored James E. Beach, turned into a home for athletics. Even a tiny triangular section at the corner of Lexington and Jones Avenues took shape as a park. Named for Lafayette, it perhaps signifies that no space is too small to give the residents of Bridgeport fresh air and happiness.

The balancing act of gray and green continued well into the twentieth century. When legions of workers' brick housing sprang up in a few short years, the architects made sure to include central greens and plots of sycamores and maples. The large Victorian houses along Park Avenue and Seaside Park continued to plant elephantine beeches and twisted basswoods. The city acquired Fayerweather Island and the swampy area west of Seaside Park in 1911, swelling the park to a magnificent 325 acres. The swamps were filled in and sand was added, increasing the beachfront. As the century progressed, the sea wall and road forged westward, connecting with the simultaneously shrinking island. Some ambitious city planners wanted to continue the road on a bridge over Black Rock Harbor, but it remained a dream. Instead, local immigrant families rowed out to the island and created a makeshift summer resort, complete with tents and cabins.

The Washington Elm on Old Mill Green was ancient but still alive when the 1938 hurricane hit the coast of New England. Hundreds of trees throughout Bridgeport were uprooted and just as quickly replaced. There was no question as to the need for this from council or voters. The colors of Bridgeport would always include brick red, soot gray and macadam black. But life-giving green would compete with them, thanks to citizens of good faith, sufficient means and strong will, who helped a gray, industrial town become known as the blessed Park City.

Chapter 8

A TALE OF TWO INVENTORS

The first decade of the twentieth century was an exciting time to live in Bridgeport. Newfangled electric trolleys rumbled over the grid of streets. Barnum and Bailey Circus still used the city for its winter quarters, and ostriches and sea lions could often be seen taking exercise in Seaside Park. Theodore Roosevelt gave a speech at the railroad station in 1905, knowing Bridgeport's huge population of immigrants would be important in the upcoming elections. Residents would soon receive access to electricity twenty-four hours a day. The world-famous Buffalo Bill lived on Railroad Avenue. It was in this atmosphere of possibility and revolution that Gustave Whitehead built his airplane.

Born in Bavaria on January 1, 1874, young Gustave got into trouble for trapping birds in nearby parks to study their method of flight. At thirteen, he even built a glider and flew it off the roof of a building in Ansbach. However, this first moonlit attempt at flight ended in a crash. Later, he learned much from the "glider king" of Germany, Otto Lillenthal, before leaving his native country for Brazil. He wandered the oceans for six years, studying seabirds and surviving four shipwrecks, until settling in the United States. Here he revived his interest in solving the problem of human flight.

Experiments with the Boston Aeronautical Society and engine work in New York were followed by marriage to Louise Tuba in Buffalo. Residence in Tonawanda, Johnstown and Pittsburgh came next, and in each place he continued to work on his airplanes and gliders. In Pittsburgh he may have achieved his first flight, but only sketchy information remains. According to a friend, Louis Davarich, he ran the engine while the inventor steered, flying half a mile before crashing into a building, breaking the steam boiler and scalding his leg. Shortly thereafter, Whitehead left with another friend for New England, stopped in Bridgeport and found work as a coal truck driver. After sending for Louise and his daughter Rose, Whitehead moved into a house at 241 Pine Street, beginning in earnest his task of constructing the "perfect airplane."

By this time, dozens of inventors had already walked the streets of Bridgeport, from Allen Wilson to Harvey Hubbell, from Waldo Calvin Bryant to Ira DeVer Warner. Louis Latimer, son of a former slave and pioneer of the electric light, spent a year here working on his devices. Bridgeport native and vice-president of the Scientific Society Charles C. Godfrey invented a private telephone line. A few had even tackled the problem of flight, like Charles F. Ritchel, inventor of the roller skate. In 1878, he built a strange hand-powered zeppelin. A rounded gas-bag made of rubber surrounded the brass frame, constructed at the nearby Folansbee Machine Shop. Ritchel could turn a drive gear that worked a propeller and steered the blimp. He took it to Hartford for a demonstration, where his assistant flew the contraption two hundred feet into the air over the Connecticut River. Featured on the cover of *Harper's Weekly*, this became the first flight of a human-powered dirigible in the United States.

Another who tackled the problem of flight was Henry House, who had worked for the Wheeler and Wilson Company and cast his first vote for Abraham Lincoln. In 1889, after a fire at his factory, House traveled to England to help build a flying machine for Hiram Maxim, inventor of the portable machine gun. House earned a variety of patents in the process, and the resulting machine showcased a surprising three hundred horsepower. Although the machine elevated briefly, House abandoned the "plane" due to its impractical tendency to catch on fire. Instead, House turned to motorboats and "horseless carriages" as more realistic applications of his time.

Flying was left to the next generation, to a mustached German immigrant with no official engineering or even mechanical training. Whitehead's efforts evolved over time, but he kept most of the work in his head. In this he did not differ much from the other inventors of the time, who often "felt" their way through the process rather than formally planning the production. Finding the right materials challenged Whitehead as well. Aluminum and balsa wood were not readily available, electrical equipment constantly short-circuited and engines had to be built on the spot rather than bought for use. Of course, Whitehead could possibly have made his job easier by aligning himself with one of the many factories in Bridgeport. In fact, he found work as a machinist at a strange new addition to the Park City, the Locomobile factory.

By the time Gustave Whitehead moved into his house in Black Rock, five thousand steam Locomobiles had already been built. Known as a reliable car, it could climb steep hills, unlike most other motorized vehicles of the

Tales from the Park City

time. In an unintentionally symbolic move, the Locomobile Company of America moved into the old Liberty Bicycle Plant, which stood on a point of land between Tongue Point Lighthouse and Seaside Park. Called "an agreeable feature of the shorefront," the plant produced five thousand steam automobiles before another inventor, Andrew Riker, changed the company forever.

Before coming to Locomobile, Andrew Riker had constructed electric vehicles, starting as a young man with an electrically driven tricycle. Founding his own company at the age of nineteen, he became the first engineer to make successful electric cars. His 1896 car became very popular in Connecticut and Long Island, driving horses crazy on the old New England roads and winning a race in New York against other electric and steam vehicles. Riker designed later models similar to a modern automobile, the first in the United States to break away from the "buggy style." But being the United States' most successful maker of electric cars wasn't enough. In his spare time, Riker developed the first four-cylinder gasoline engine and sold it to Locomobile. In 1901, he moved to Bridgeport to design a whole line of them, two years before the organization of Ford Motor Company. The first gasoline-powered Locomobile, a four-cylinder, chain-drive, three-speed vehicle, went to M.M. Riglander of New York in 1902.

Andrew Riker had applied his genius to a problem and used the financial and material support of this flourishing company to do so. But although Gustave Whitehead received support from a menagerie of fascinated backers over the years, he never allied himself with Locomobile or another factory. It could be that none showed interest in the project at this prenatal stage of "aeroplane" development. Or it could be that Whitehead simply did not work well with others. He certainly drove what backers he had away with his careless attitudes toward money and time. Many left in disgust when they found him working on other projects or taking too long to complete "their" work.

Poorly funded, this was a home-grown operation. Louise sewed the wings to the frame while her husband attached his propellers to boats and tried them out in Black Rock Harbor. Whitehead built his own motors, a feat untried by any other early airplane inventors. He even used a Locomobile car to tow the planes into the air and measure the thrust requirements of the engine. Sometimes he tested them on Pine Street in the early morning, and numerous witness accounts remain of these "hops." Joseph Ratzenberger, a policeman, remembered a summer flight in which Whitehead traveled down the entire street to Bostwick Avenue at a height of twelve feet above the ground. John Ciglar recalled a similar flight that ended in a crash and

BRIDGEPORT

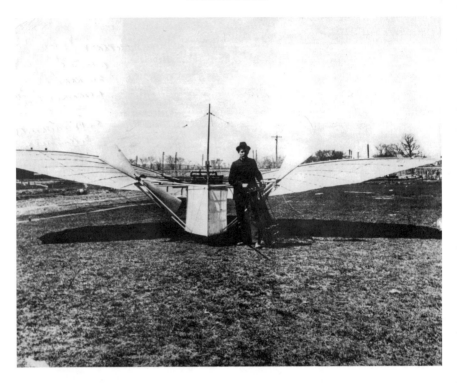

After constructing over fifty prototypes, Gustave Whitehead got off the ground with "Number 21" four times on August 14, 1901. *Courtesy of the Bridgeport Public Library Historical Collections.*

a burst of flames. Others described journeys of hundreds of feet at heights ranging from four to fifteen feet above the ground, after which Whitehead would calculate errors and improve his designs. While these may not seem impressive, they easily equaled the Wright brothers' celebrated first flights.

Two days make Whitehead's story significant: August 14, 1901, and January 17, 1902. In 1901, he made his attempt with a plane he called Number 21, though it was actually his fifty-sixth model. He took the plane over the border of Fairfield to Tunxis Hill at dawn and flew the plane for a half mile. The 30-foot canvas wings had trouble hauling the heavy white pine and bamboo body of the plane but held. Heartened by this "partial success," as he called it, he made three more flights the same day, one of which a witness reported to be a mile and a half. Whitehead came back and told his wife that "we went up." The *New York Herald* and *Boston Transcript* reported on the event, and that week's *Bridgeport Sunday Herald* included an eyewitness account. This was over two years before the Wrights forced their contraption into the air at Kitty Hawk for a mere 852 feet.

Tales from the Park City

A few months later, in January, Whitehead took a new plane, Number 22, to Lordship Manor, where he made two flights, the second of which was reported to be an astonishing seven miles. The plane used a forty-horsepower kerosene engine that he had pared down to 120 pounds. Unlike Number 21, this plane used mostly steel and aluminum for its frame and silk for its wings. The lighter plane easily took off without the use of an incline, traveled out over the blue waters of Long Island Sound and circled over the harbor. Whitehead built the fuselage to be water-tight, and after landing in the water, his assistants towed him to shore.

His assistants, Junius Harworth and Anton Pruckner, later signed affidavits swearing that they, along with many others, witnessed the flights. Both *Scientific American* and the *Aeronautic World* published extensive details about the Bridgeport man's planes. Nevertheless, no one took a stopwatch and timed the flights. More distressingly, no photographs were taken, or at least Whitehead kept none himself. Perfectionist that he was, he remained dissatisfied with these flights, though they far exceeded the imagination of the public of the time.

Meanwhile, under Andrew Riker's direction, gas-powered cars improved by leaps and bounds. The engine increased to six cylinders, incorporated a shaft drive and added a speed to its transmission. Riker himself solved the problem of clutch construction. Another Bridgeport company, Raybestos, soon helped these developments. Formed in 1904, it fabricated brake linings and clutch facings that proved vital to the safety of these new automobiles. It became possibly the first company to perform large-scale testing of its product in action. Almost every car manufacturer used Raybestos, and Locomobile was no exception.

A young Walter Chrysler saw one of Riker's new Locomobiles at the Chicago Auto Show in 1905 and fell in love. Using his life savings of $700 and borrowing a further $4,300, he bought it. But Chrysler didn't want to parade the sparkling white vehicle with its plush red upholstery in front of his friends and neighbors. He laboriously took it apart and put it back together again, teaching himself how a "motorcar" worked. It would serve him well in his future success in the automobile industry.

Then, in 1908, the esteemed Vanderbilt Cup Contest fell to a Locomobile. The car, called "No. 16," clocked a new record average speed of 64.38 miles per hour. Riker's car became the first American automobile to take the exalted European award. However, luxury, not speed, distinguished Locomobile. Riker continued to insist on the highest standards, and sometimes produced only four cars per day due to the quality control he instituted. "As fine as could be made" was Locomobile's motto. New York decorator Elsie Dewolfe

Bridgeport

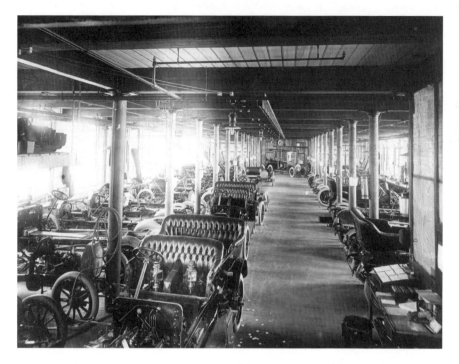

First producing steam-engine cars, the Locomobile Company began building gasoline-powered models in 1901. *Courtesy of the Bridgeport Public Library Historical Collections.*

selected upholstery while Tiffany and Company supplied silver fittings for ornamentation. Locomobile also established a "custom" line of cars for the wealthy families of Boston and New York, adding silk upholstery, loudspeakers and reading lamps. A Locomobile achieved the distinction of "Car of 1911" and "Car of 1912" in *Yearbooks Illustrated*.

During World War I, Locomobile built thousands of "Riker Trucks" for England's beleaguered soldiers. In 1915, Thomas Edison himself chose Andrew Riker for President Woodrow Wilson's Naval Advisory Board. At his suggestion, the Locomobile factory assembled the famous staff cars and trucks used by General Pershing. It also designed and built a forty-ton tank with two six-pound guns and seven machine guns, but the war ended before it was shipped to the French front.

After Andrew Riker left the Locomobile Company, it went through several owners, fighting bankruptcy and buyouts. General Motors attempted to restructure the company, including production of a line of taxicabs. But the Great Depression was the death knell for small auto makers like Locomobile, and its doors closed in 1930. Riker himself was long gone, of course, a

Tales from the Park City

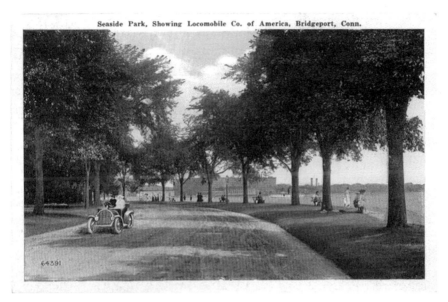

The luxurious Locomobile was the perfect vehicle for sunlit drives through Seaside Park. *Courtesy of the Bridgeport Public Library Historical Collections.*

success by any stretch of the imagination. His son went on to invent a home screen for movies and slides and manage the Pratt-Whitney Aircraft plant in Meriden, a job one might have imagined for Gustave Whitehead.

Of course, after the incredible flights of 1901 and 1902, Whitehead was not finished. He continued to try to improve his planes without steady funding or support. He also continued to build motors for planes and boats. He perfected his unpowered aircraft, and many sunny summer days on Tunxis Hill in nearby Fairfield included a ride in one of "Gus Whitehead's gliders." Young boys from the neighborhood helped the strange man with the German accent run these contraptions down the hill and send them airborne. Some also stopped in his workshop and helped him with his constructions, and a few found professional work in later life on the strength of the skills they learned with him.

A man named Buffalo Jones, hero of a Zane Grey book, actually financed a small helicopter project, which Whitehead gladly completed. Then, in 1911, Whitehead's fortunes took a dreadful turn when an entrepreneur, Lee Burridge, financed a larger project. Whitehead got far enough to build the first helicopter model and labor on the second. However, he and Burridge had a falling out, as the eccentric immigrant did with so many of his backers. This time Burridge sued him for not completing the contract and seized the contents of his workshop. It proved to be the final straw, and Whitehead never experimented with airplanes again.

In his last years, an eye injury from a steel chip worsened and a delicate heart began to fail him. World War I caused a surge of anti-German feeling and Whitehead blamed it for the lack of credit for his work. It is more likely, however, that Whitehead's own mechanical perfectionism caused his downfall. At one point he told Anton Pruckner, his assistant, "All these flights are not much good, because they don't last long enough. We just cannot fly to any old place. Flight will only then become of importance, when we can fly at any time to any given place." This insistence on perfection, on this fastidious definition of flight, seems to have stopped him from realizing and trumpeting his own achievement.

By understanding that invention was progressive rather than a sudden success, Andrew Riker established his place in a long line of engineers who made automobile travel possible. The story of powered flight worked the same way, of course, but has often been boiled down to one spectacular triumph—the Wright brothers. This seems a strange anomaly, especially since the Wrights built on previous knowledge. In fact, they may have visited Whitehead himself. In Anton Pruckner's sworn affidavit, he stated: "I can also remember very clearly when the Wright brothers visited Whitehead's shop here in Bridgeport before 1903. I was present and saw them myself. I know this to be true, because they introduced themselves to me at the time. In no way am I confused as some people have felt with the Wittemann brothers who came here after 1906. I knew Charles Wittemann well. The Wrights left here with a great deal of information." Of course, whether they learned anything is unknown, and their biplane certainly looked nothing like Whitehead's, which much more resembled the aircraft of today.

To exacerbate the problem for historians, the Bridgeport inventor's gadgets, plans and other notes disappeared, taken to the dump by disappointed relatives. They also donated his remaining engines to wartime scrap metal drives. Was it simply a lack of understanding of proper documentation that led to his downfall? Dozens of photographs of the planes exist, but in-flight photos have never turned up. Though over thirty people signed affidavits that they had seen the planes in flight, apparently this did not satisfy the new reliance on graphic evidence. Was the Wrights' success based partly on their cleverness at filming their attempts? Or on their experimental persistence and ability to sell their talents to sponsors?

It is a story that can make the reader question all of history, of how things become acceptable to record keepers, to the public, to culture itself. The usually methodical Smithsonian Institute did not help the controversy when

Tales from the Park City

it signed a contract with the Wright brothers stating that it would never consider proof of any previous flights, including those possibly made by its own previous director, Samuel Langley. If nothing else, North Carolina's license plate logo tells us that this piece of history is not going anywhere soon. One imagines that if Whitehead had the late P.T. Barnum as his publicist and champion, facts in textbooks might be much different today.

And yet, if we open a German history book to the origins of air travel, we find something remarkable. The Wright brothers are just a note, and Gustav Weisskopf is championed as "Erster Motorflug der Welt," the world's first person to achieve powered flight. Perhaps that victory would have satisfied Whitehead. But whatever its judgment, history was a long way off for the Bridgeport aeronaut, and he died of a heart attack in 1927, a disenchanted and deeply discouraged man.

Chapter 9

TEXTBOOKS AND TOOTHACHES

The adults were the worst. A good day at the office involved cysts, exposed pulps and inflamed gums. These people were in great pain and needed extractions, fillings and sympathy. But by the time they came to Dr. Fones, the battle with tooth decay was lost. All he did was rip out the rotten ones. Could this really be the job of a dentist? Yanking dead molars, he did little more than act as a glorified funeral director.

Alfred Fones was born in Bridgeport in 1869. His father, Civilion Fones, actually served as mayor of the city in 1886 and 1887 and had known P.T. Barnum well. He was also a practicing dentist and the first dental commissioner for the city of Bridgeport. For Alfred, it seemed natural to go into his father's business, and he attended the New York College of Dentistry. Upon graduation, he returned to Bridgeport and set up his practice on the corner of State and Myrtle Avenues, in the back of the office where his father worked. By the turn of the century, he realized the importance of the prevention of oral disease for patients, the community and the world.

Others had had this notion, to be sure. Dr. Wright of Cincinnati, Ohio, had given a lecture on a similar idea that Fones had heard at a conference in 1899. He had been so impressed that he observed Wright's clinic, finding the patients far healthier than his own. In addition, Dr. Low of Buffalo had suggested "Odontocure," in which a woman with an orange wooden stick, pumice and a flannel rag would make rounds in a neighborhood twice a month to clean and polish teeth. Only a few years before, the same year Fones graduated from dental school, Willoughby D. Miller had discovered that bacteria caused tooth decay. If that was the case, then why not work to combat those bacteria? Why not stop the decay in teeth before it started, rather than acting as an undertaker?

Fones decided that he would actually put this radical idea into practice and would call it "dental hygiene." No doubt he would encounter resistance.

Tales from the Park City

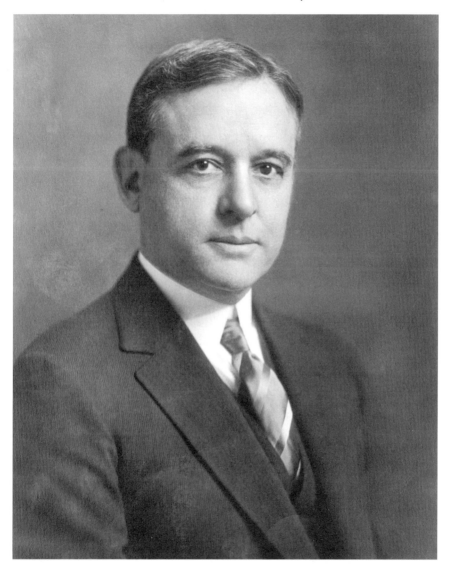

Dr. Alfred Fones, having witnessed the perils of tooth decay, revolutionized the care of teeth. *Courtesy of the Fones School of Dental Hygiene.*

The ideas of keeping the mouth clean and preventing disease seemed crazy in a field where extractions were the rule for dental problems. However, he found that the main problem with this idea proved to be time. A practicing dentist simply had no time to clean the teeth of every patient.

To combat this, Dr. Fones tried something quite new, adopting the use of a "hygienist" in his practice. Fones's cousin and chair-side assistant, Irene

Bridgeport

Newman, agreed to learn to clean teeth under his guidance. As he began to teach Irene, Alfred realized he would need to have teaching aids. He mounted extracted teeth in a modeling compound. Then, painting plaster of Paris around the necks of the teeth, he artfully simulated calculus. Irene carefully polished off this fabricated tartar, along with indelible ink the dentist stained onto the teeth. She learned quickly, and Alfred became convinced that they were on the right track.

Meanwhile, they had left his father's building to set up his practice at a big, brick carriage house on Washington Street. Over the garage, reception rooms and labs offered space for clients and research, while private offices above gave them room to plan the future. It was here, in 1907, that Irene Newman first performed the duties we now associate with preventative tooth care. Irene was about to become the world's first dental hygienist. But before any real change could take effect, Dr. Fones had to educate the public and his fellow dentists. His friends tried to dissuade him. Dentists from elsewhere wrote articles against it. They upheld the idea as foolhardy and promised his ruin. They assured him that no patients would actually pay for "regular checkups." In any other city, this might have been the case, but in Bridgeport, such "crazy" ideas were commonplace. And Dr. Fones had worked hard to prepare the community: writing articles, giving demonstrations and persuading his patients one at a time.

The hard work paid off, and his patients returned at regular intervals of six months. An examination cost ten cents, a cleaning twenty-five and any of the traditional surgical procedures another quarter. The benefits of periodic dental prophylaxis quickly became apparent to both the patients and Fones. Dental professionals traveled from New Haven and New York to visit this "modern edifice of oral health care." This new idea attracted attention and support. A question came just as naturally as the first one Fones had ten years earlier: why not teach others this method? Why not start a school?

Finally, by 1913, the hardworking Dr. Fones collected $46,000 in funds and donations. In the rear of the carriage house, the school took shape, with just enough space for everyone to practice the techniques on each other. The old garage on the first floor housed a lecture hall and the cellar became the practice area. Thirty-four women jumped at the opportunity to take that first class, enrolling in numerous courses such as tooth anatomy, histology and clinical practice. Already schoolteachers, nurses and doctors' wives, many students started the classes with an eye to expand their skills. Even Mrs. Fones attended the class, saying that her husband was so busy it was the only way she could see him. Dr. Fones encouraged each student: "Be courteous, be understanding and read, read, read!"

Tales from the Park City

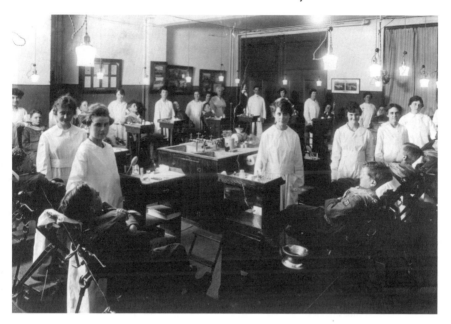

A class of dental hygienists prepares to practice on the local Boy Scout troop. *Courtesy of the Fones School of Dental Hygiene.*

As the first year of classes sped by, local Bridgeport dentists gave free lectures. Quickly, the faculty expanded to include the deans of the dental schools of Pennsylvania and Harvard, seven professors from Yale and two from Columbia. Fones even brought in a few professionals from Japan. Courses such as pathology and bacteriology were fully illustrated by pictures and slides using a balopticon and a screen. Once recorded and compiled, these lectures became the first dental hygienist textbook, called *Mouth Hygiene*.

In the cellar of the carriage house, Irene Newman demonstrated and the students followed her lead. They practiced their trade on manikin heads, complete with rubber cheeks, tongues and two full sets of teeth and movable jaws. Newman attached these heads to the green chairs in place of headrests, each illuminated by an electric droplight. In the center of the room was a zinc table with running hot and cold water, powdered pumice and alcohol. Students sterilized their instruments by dipping them into a large vat of water, which boiled and bubbled cheerily.

These budding hygienists took the next step by cleaning neighborhood children's teeth. Boy Scout troops marched in, and the students removed tartar and stains, polishing each tooth. They used dental floss dipped in fine powdered pumice to get in between, noting the problem areas to point out to the dentist who supervised them. Fones and Newman also used these opportunities to spread the gospel of proper home care and diet to the community. This built on a program started in 1909 that Fones had begun as president of the Bridgeport Dental Society.

The first women graduated and were ready to practice in June 1915. Many went on to jobs with the Bridgeport school district, where they played a significant role in reducing dental disease in schoolchildren by 75 percent. Their duties included teaching students about the dangers of too much sugar and candy. Before the program, each child averaged seven cavities apiece. Bridgeport soon gained fame for its community oral hygiene and became the starting point for similar programs across the country and the world. In 1917, Connecticut passed its earliest law licensing these hygienists and handed the first to Irene Newman. Many of these women spread out across the United States to pioneer the techniques and skills in new cities. Some ran into opposition, and one student was actually thrown in jail for practicing "dental hygiene."

Meanwhile, the terrible influenza epidemic that swept the world during World War I hit the Park City. Most cities closed schools, but in Bridgeport

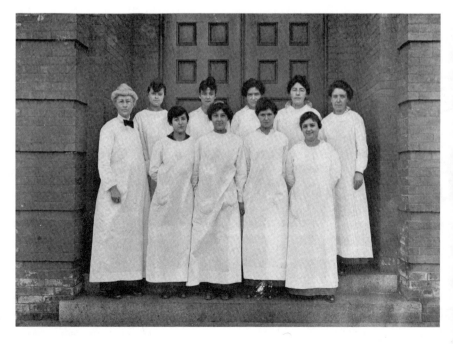

The world's first dental hygienist, Irene Newman, poses with her class in 1914. *Courtesy of the Fones School of Dental Hygiene.*

they were kept open, escalating the instruction of food and hygiene principles already in place. The city health officer expanded this campaign to theatres and public facilities. As a result, Bridgeport had the lowest known death rate of any large city in America—only one half of 1 percent.

The successful Dr. Fones often spent his vacations at a summer camp on the Housatonic River near New Milford. He often walked with his old friend, E. Everett Cortright, on the rolling green hills above the river. They discussed Cortright's ideas for education in Bridgeport on their walks, on the golf course and over games of bridge. Cortright fumed over a new Census Bureau report that showed Bridgeport with the lowest per capita number of college-bound students. Their talks generated new ideas and new visions. These two friends were about to change Bridgeport forever.

E. Everett Cortright was born in Middletown, New York, and became a schoolteacher before his eighteenth birthday. With a paycheck of seven dollars per week, he saved enough money to attend college, alternating studying and teaching for a number of years. He came to Bridgeport to teach physics and mathematics at the city high school and eventually was promoted to superintendant of schools. After a short stint as a professor at NYU, where he studied the "junior college" idea in depth, Cortright came back to the Park City with a firm idea that higher education should be democratized. "Ability and leadership in America must be sought in all groups," he stated in the *Bridgeport Post*.

In his research at NYU, Cortright had found that Bridgeport was one of only six American cities of 100,000 people with no institute of higher education. Moreover, college-bound students in the East usually arrived only from the upper strata of society. With this in mind, the former schoolteacher gave passionate speeches and entered debates on the importance of the junior college idea with the chamber of commerce, local women's groups and the deans and presidents of other universities. "The democratic sentiment demands every group be served," he told them. "Man has learned more about the world in the past half century than in all the preceding centuries put together." So, he asked them, how can this knowledge be passed down?

The answer was a two-year junior college system. The president of Harvard, Laurence Lowell, agreed with Cortright publicly, stating that universities were wasting time teaching subjects that should have been taught in high school. He contended that continued specialization of university courses had led to a lack of general courses, the important ones universities had taught for hundreds of years. The newspapers in Bridgeport and surrounding towns asked the citizens, "Do you believe there is a place for such an institution in Bridgeport?" The answer was a resounding yes.

Bridgeport

After a fateful summit at the Brooklawn Country Club with Fones and Raybestos president and local philanthropist Sumner Simpson, a determined Cortright began several years of organizational activities. Fones himself secured a new building for the school at 1001 Fairfield Avenue with $30,000 of his own money. The tapestry brick and Indiana limestone building would accommodate three hundred students, and plans were made for seven hundred more. Inside, the old woodwork was painted and finished in eggshell enamel. Terrazzo rooms were furnished with heavy opera chairs and converted into a chemistry lab, locker rooms, a library and nine classrooms. This humble building would be the home of the city's first college.

Of course, they needed people to teach classes and run the school. Cortright made personal appeals to qualified teachers throughout the community and abroad. He actually walked the streets of Bridgeport, at one point knocking on the door of Margaret McEnerny's house on Norman Street and hiring her as his secretary. He hired Dr. Helen Scurr, a Shakespearean scholar and a collector of rare books, to teach literature and writing. She lent her Tolstoy and Dostoyevsky to students, encouraging them to read. "Great books grow on you," she said. Cortright also persuaded the former college roommate of Benito Mussolini, Professor Pierre Zampierre, to teach French, though he could have taught any of his seven other languages.

The Junior College of Connecticut's charter was signed on May 5, 1927, barely two years after Cortright had first made the idea public. The city's papers raved about this new addition to the community, and its success would spawn fourteen more junior colleges throughout the region over the next few years. Fones was elected to be the head of the board of trustees and Cortright became the college president. The following February, twenty-eight day and forty-seven evening students joined the eleven faculty and staff members. They started with thirty-four evening classes, including such seeming anomalies as basic Hungarian, elements of aeronautics and industrial management. Of course, in Bridgeport, these subjects seemed natural and right.

The students who came to this new, affordable school often came as "commuters," a strange new development. The American education system was changing, and college was not just for the "elite." Nevertheless, Fones and Cortright committed to giving these students a comprehensive education. They brought in speakers like Bridgeport mayor Jasper McLevy, who gave a lecture on "What Socialism Means Today as a Method of Government," speaking about evolution versus revolution. Cortright himself gave a talk on Roosevelt's New Deal, explaining that as America changed, it needed to assist "the man who had often been exploited." The Great Depression

Tales from the Park City

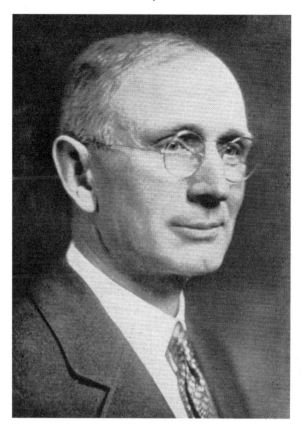

Dr. E. Everett Cortright developed the first junior college in New England in 1927. *Courtesy of the University of Bridgeport Archives.*

and women's suffrage had changed the cultural map of the United States, and Bridgeport was now a place for the discussion of cutting-edge issues. Women entered the Junior College of Connecticut with fresh dreams. Mary Birmingham, who "abhorred" housework, signed up in 1933 with plans to become a surgeon. It was a progressive school for a progressing world.

The college added dormitories, and Arnold College from New Haven joined the Junior College. Cortright continued his involvement, addressing and getting to know incoming freshmen and meeting with junior college executives from across the country. Board meetings and talks jammed his schedule. As chairman of the board of trustees, Fones awarded degrees at graduation, sending students off to jobs or four-year schools. Colleges like Wellesley, Barnard and Columbia praised the students of the Junior College for their skills and preparedness.

In 1935, despite the Great Depression, the School of Business opened. Bridgeport businessmen now taught classes in a city with more international commerce per person than any in the country. Once again, Cortright secured funds and convinced the public of the viability of the idea. The robust health of the Junior College made the argument easier. However, at sixty-two years old, Cortright's own health was failing. Even so, he was unprepared when, in 1938, Alfred Fones died while watching a movie in a Main Street theatre. An attendant noted that he had apparently fallen asleep, but he could not stir him. The famous dentist was buried later that week at Mountain Grove Cemetery, near P.T. Barnum himself.

After World War II, veterans flocked to the Junior College on the new GI Bill. Many saw this as a temporary bubble, but the new president, James Halsey, with the advice of Cortright, now on the board of trustees, decided it was the opening they needed to become a full university. Petitions from students, many of them veterans, helped sway local and state opinion to this end. In 1947, the creation of the University of Bridgeport offered "to provide guidance to living, to help the student realize his capabilities as a rational man or woman capable of meeting the moral, social, economic, and emotional problems of life." The new university moved to its present Seaside Park campus, having purchased P.T. Barnum's Marina mansion and nearby properties a few years earlier.

The two thousand students could walk to the beach, and most had views of Long Island Sound from their windows. Huge beech and basswood trees shaded the lawns of the beautiful new campus. The enormous Perry Arch that led into Seaside Park became a symbol of the school, and the students quickly adopted the unique park as their own. Victorian and turn-of-the-century manors became dormitories for the thousands of new scholars, as well as the sites of their club meetings, tea dances and balls. They debated topics like civil rights. Their paintings were displayed in venues throughout the city. In short, they filled the south end of Bridgeport with new energy and imagination.

Cortright honored his old friend with the first new academic building erected, named Fones Memorial Hall. The Fones School of Dental Hygiene also officially opened at the University of Bridgeport, creating revolution again. It would be the first school of dental hygiene attached to a university in the world. Some dentists were suspicious that hygienists could be properly prepared in a "college" setting rather than at a dental school, but its immediate success silenced them. The dreams of Alfred Fones and E. Everett Cortright had come full circle.

Bridgeport had always been a place for pioneers. Now, it was set to teach others to follow their dreams. Still alive at mid-century, the world's first dental hygienist, Irene Newman, gave an interview about her part in this great saga of education. With characteristic forthrightness and modesty, she summed up the entire philosophy of her home city: "I didn't think a thing of it. The work was there to do and I did it."

Chapter 10

ARSENAL OF A NATION

Henry Mucci was born in 1911 to an Italian immigrant family. They had joined the huge boom in immigration at the turn of the century that made Bridgeport even more of an "international city." Any newsstand sold papers printed in Italian, Hungarian, German, Yiddish and Slovak. Henry attended grammar school in Bridgeport before applying to West Point, where he was initially rejected due to being "short" on physical requirements. This was an ironic outcome for a man who would not only be legendary for his physical fitness but would also become one of the greatest heroes of World War II.

Henry's childhood in Bridgeport during the First World War no doubt inspired his rise to military fame. He may have walked past the squat, intimidating guardhouses at the Remington factory. Perhaps he knew they protected the largest factory in the entire world, which at its peak employed twenty thousand people and stretched a half-mile long. It began producing munitions for the Europeans in 1915, eventually increasing to 100,000 rifles per month and 10,000 bayonets per day. Remington produced the Browning machine gun, the Colt automatic pistol and seven million rounds of ammunition a week, two thirds of all the American-made ammunition used for Allied forces.

The luxury car factory of the Locomobile Company built trucks for the English forces. The Bridgeport Brass Company, the American and British Manufacturing Company and the American Tube and Stamping Company all pushed out parts and weapons for the war. In less than one year, the population of the town increased radically, as fifty thousand people flooded in to work in the factories. This forced Remington to build extensive employee housing, and the Bridgeport Housing Company erected one thousand new homes. At the huge munitions factory, men crafted shot and lead bullets, stuffed powder and used bulky stamping contraptions. Coming from New

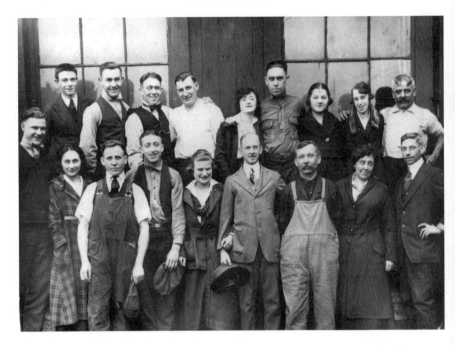

A group of factory workers take a moment to relax outside the American Tube and Stamping Company in 1920. *Courtesy of Joseph E. Nechasek.*

York to take advantage of the spike in jobs, women tended cartridge-making and trimming machines.

Not all this work went smoothly. Exploited union machinists randomly stopped work, deaf to patriotic appeals. Hearings ensued and protests continued. President Woodrow Wilson actually threatened to void the workers' military exceptions in order to stop the strikes. However, as demand for jobs went down, thousands joined the unions to make sure that they shared in the profits of this booming economy. By the end of the war, an eight-hour workday was won.

The most fascinating place that young Henry could have imagined in those war years would have been the Simon Lake Torpedo Boat Company. Simon Lake's childhood had been very different from Henry's. His entire family had been inventors, crafting useful gear like the whistling buoy, seed-planting machine and window shade rollers. However, his mother died when he was only three, leaving him in the hands of his step-grandmother, who read to him from the Bible and did not hesitate to punish him severely. He had no friends and endured daily fights. Then, Simon's life changed when he read Jules Verne's *Twenty Thousand Leagues Under the Sea*. He conducted experiments based on this book, becoming obsessed with the idea of building an "under-sea boat." Figuring out human oxygen requirements was the biggest problem he encountered. After searching through all the available data and consulting experts, Simon was still stumped. So the boy enclosed himself in a box for one hour, calculating the volume of air per hour a person required and finding that you could re-breathe air at least twice.

By fourteen, Simon had the plans for his submarine. It would be a few years before he got backers and built the *Argonaut* of his dream. The navy was impressed but not convinced. The competing Electric Boat Company tried to put them out of business, but it didn't work. Lake's underwater boats dispatched to Austria and Russia instead. Finally, the inventor moved to Bridgeport and formed his company on Seaview Avenue, building the *Protector* right in the Pequonnock River. The vessel was smaller and could be used for coastal defense, causing demand for it to soar.

During the war, a stouter and wiser Lake bought more "water lots" and expanded the factory, quadrupling production to twenty submarines a year and selling to the U.S. Navy and its allies. The young naval secretary, Franklin Delano Roosevelt, came to town and inspected Lake's work, as well as the naval base at Black Rock and Remington Arms. The inventor could often be seen poring over his employees' work, squinting through an eye injured working on the periscope. He tallied over 1,500 patents, 111 on submarines alone. Airlocks, steering gears and prefabricated houses all owe a debt to Lake's tireless ingenuity. But most importantly, in his years in Bridgeport, Simon Lake changed the submarine from a suicidal machine to the most feared vessel in the world.

As well as being the "arsenal of the nation," Bridgeport bequeathed nearly nine thousand of its citizens to fight in the First World War. The city was ahead of the curve, anticipating that war would be declared and organizing several companies. On July 24, 1917, a military parade occupied the streets and marched past cheering families, escorted by Home Guard units. Early the next morning, the soldiers broke camp at their mobilization point at Pleasure Beach. The railroad station platforms creaked with the weight of the waving families, friends and girlfriends of the soldiers. Women fainted and men struggled to hide tears.

No doubt a young Henry Mucci felt inspired by these soldiers, who distinguished themselves in both the navy and the army. The First Connecticut Ambulance Corps, known as "Bridgeport's Own," became instrumental on the western front of France. Henry may have been especially encouraged by the example of war heroes like John MacKenzie. Born in Bridgeport in 1886, MacKenzie joined the navy in 1902 and attained the rate of coxswain before

Bridgeport

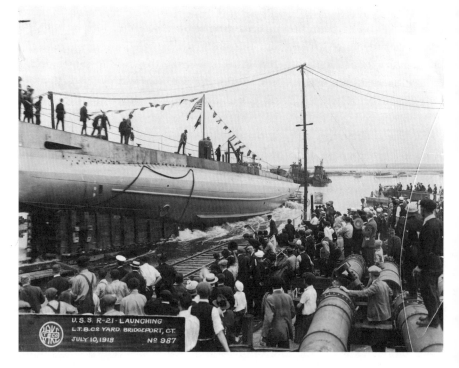

Simon Lake's USS *R-21* submarine launches in Bridgeport during World War I. *Courtesy of the Bridgeport Public Library Historical Collections.*

discharging in 1907. In 1917, when the United States entered World War I, MacKenzie reenlisted, serving onboard the USS *Remlik* as chief boatswain's mate. During a dangerous storm off the coast of France, a depth charge became loose on deck and could have blown up, possibly sinking the ship. MacKenzie risked his life to save the crew and vessel and won the Medal of Honor.

A total of 237 Bridgeporters never returned from the Great War, and their names were etched into a marble tablet on the city hall green. On Armistice Day, all the church bells in the city rang. Cannon in Seaside Park boomed and factory whistles blew. With the usual Bridgeport grandiosity, a spontaneous parade spilled into the streets, including factory workers carrying flags, bands of playing musicians, decorated automobiles and even farm wagons. Windows exploded with red, white and blue drapes. Confetti snowed down from the office buildings. A twenty-four-hour party ensued, two days before the "official" parade marched through town. Approximately 100,000 spectators lined up to watch two and a half hours of procession passing by. School students marched behind the high school band, and perhaps little Henry joined them.

Tales from the Park City

In 1927, the Barnum and Bailey Circus, now a property of the Ringling Brothers, moved its winter quarters to Florida. The Wall Street crash of 1929 followed, annihilating the city's economy, and Bridgeport factories spent a decade suffering. Meanwhile, Mucci attended West Point, where he boxed, played lacrosse and shot basketballs. He also became a crack shot with his rifle and charmed everyone he met. Graduating in 1936, he served in Texas and Wyoming before being shipped out to Hawaii. There he would be provost marshal in Honolulu during the dastardly attack on Pearl Harbor that dragged the United States into World War II.

Once again, Bridgeport's industrious and inventive nature would be tested. One of those who rose to the challenge was Edwin Herbert Land, two years ahead of Henry Mucci in school. After growing up in the Park City, he attended Harvard University but quit for a time to invent a new type of light polarizer. Along with a group of other young scientists, he worked on applying the principle to all sorts of optical devices, including film. The Polaroid Corporation was born in 1937, with Land both researching and acting as president. During the war, he geared the research toward martial apparatus, inventing infrared filters, dark-adaptation goggles and target finders. Afterward he would go on to introduce his famous camera, which of course was also called the Polaroid.

But the most important and world-changing inventor in Bridgeport during World War II was an immigrant. Igor Sikorsky grew up in Kiev, Russia, in a house full of books. Like Simon Lake, he loved Jules Verne, and the story *The Clipper of the Clouds* inspired his dreams of taking to the skies. At age ten, he studied Leonardo da Vinci's drawings and speculations, and he built a small spring-driven helicopter in 1899. Sikorsky entered the Polytechnic Institute of Kiev in 1907, at a time when the Russians were still using balloons for military reconnaissance. He designed elementary airplanes, though he failed to perfect a helicopter at this early date. Emperor Nicholas II personally met Sikorsky and inspected his flying machines.

The inventor continued to improve his designs until the Bolshevik revolution, when he escaped to New York, forced to start over in a land where no one knew of his successes. He branched out and created amphibious planes, or "flying boats," as they were called. His S-38 sold like hotcakes to all commercial, business and military airlines, dominating the "golden age of amphibious flying boats." Still, Sikorsky's dreams of vertical flight were still unfinished. During the Second World War, he moved operations to Bridgeport and nearby Stratford, intent on building the first working helicopter.

Sikorsky noted that the "difficulty was threefold" in surpassing the few clunky, short-lived and limited machines that existed at the time. "First, we

BRIDGEPORT

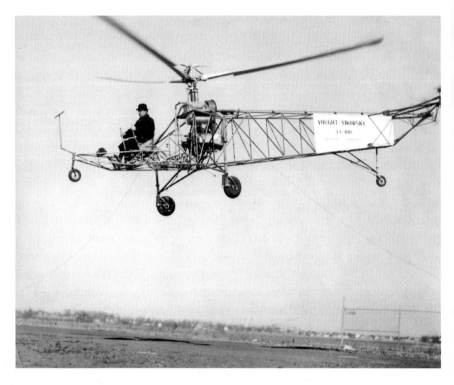

Igor Sikorsky piloting one of his VS-300 helicopters during World War II. *Courtesy of the Bridgeport Public Library Historical Collections.*

had little knowledge of helicopters in general; second, we were building the first helicopter in the world with a single main rotor; and third, we knew practically nothing about how to pilot a helicopter." These were formidable challenges, to say the least. But on May 6, 1941, Sikorsky piloted the world helicopter flight endurance record with a time of one hour and thirty-two minutes. Huge numbers of spectators and reporters watched the event, and subsequently, Sikorsky meant "helicopter" to the American public.

His engineer, William Hunt, said that Sikorsky's best characteristic was "his remarkable resilience in the face of tremendous odds." The Russian inventor had recreated his career three times, and the last revision was about to take him into the annals of American history. The VS-300 spun out in its final form on the day after Pearl Harbor. In 1942, Sikorsky gave a lecture at the University of Bridgeport on this new breed of flying machines, focusing on its usefulness in rescue missions. Unlike his Bridgeport antecedent in flying machines, Gustave Whitehead, Sikorsky knew exactly how to sell his ideas and products, and he turned his prodigious skills on the U.S. military.

Tales from the Park City

In 1943, the U.S. Navy began buying Sikorsky's helicopters, following a test flight in Bridgeport by a Coast Guard lieutenant commander named F.A. Erickson. The world's first helicopter assembly line sprang up on South Avenue. Hundreds of VS-300s joined the war effort, as well as over one hundred R-4s and R-5s, used as rescue vehicles for the navy and beyond. On November 29, 1945, Sikorsky test pilot Jimmy Viner and Captain Jackson Beighle of the air force steered an R-5 into heavy rain and sixty-mile-an-hour winds off the coast of Bridgeport. With a new hydraulic hoist attached to the helicopter, they rescued two men from a wrecked barge on Penfield Reef. Sikorsky's vertical flying machine, once only in the imagination of a small Russian boy, would transform both lifesaving and war in the century to come.

Meanwhile, Bridgeport's citizens had also been called to war, and this time Henry Mucci was among them. His brother John had been sent as a combat engineer to the Italian campaign, but Henry served in the Pacific. By 1944, he found himself in Port Moresby, New Guinea, with a new job, training the Sixth Ranger Battalion. They had been "mule skinners," large farmers and ranchers who carried howitzers. After their assignment in New Guinea, the mules were sent to Burma and the unit was disbanded. It reformed under the command of this "Little MacArthur," who smoked a pipe and sported a thin little mustache. For one year in the mountains of New Guinea, Mucci personally educated his team, one of the first American special operations fighting forces.

At first, the team hated Mucci. Short and muscular, his incredible physical shape allowed him to outmarch all his men, pushing them to the absolute limits of their capacities. He personally taught them all aspects of fighting: hand-to-hand combat, knifing, bayoneting and marksmanship. He led them on torturous exercises across the tropical New Guinea jungles, through treacherous rivers with full packs and up mountainsides in the ferocious heat. He employed dramatic schemes, using motivational gimmicks and "coyote teaching" with his men. The soldiers would approach him with a knife and he would toss them on their backs using judo. John Richardson, Sixth Army ranger, recalled: "I wondered why he was putting us through so much, but before it was over, there was no question about it, I knew why. And once he got us trained and picked out, he loved us to death. And there wasn't anything too good for us...He *knew* what he was doing when he was training us." Once he got the men trained to a lethal perfection, this "tough cookie" softened up, and his men became incredibly loyal. As Robert Prince, captain of the company Mucci took to Cabanatuan, said, "We knew he was selling us the blue sky, but we would have followed him anywhere."

Bridgeport

Early in the war, American forces that surrendered to the Japanese in the Philippines had been marched to Cabanatuan City. Along the way, more than 15,000 people were murdered on the three-day "Bataan Death March"; 10,000 survived and some eventually dispersed to other camps. But only 513 of the remaining 3,000 had survived the terrible conditions of Cabanatuan. Now these survivors were in danger, as well. The War Ministry in Japan had sent a directive that came to be called the infamous "August 1 Kill-All Order." The prisons throughout the Japanese-held islands would be disposed of. By the time General MacArthur took the greatest fleet to ever sail the Pacific and landed a huge force in the Philippines, the prisoners at Palawan Island, southwest of Bataan, had already been massacred.

The United States military decided to mount a rescue operation, and it called on Lieutenant Colonel Henry Mucci. Part of the invasion of Leyte in October 1944, the Rangers had secured three small islands. But they had little to actually do. Now was their chance to prove the effectiveness of Mucci's training. Not only would it be a prison break of epic proportions, but it would also be a rescue of the famed Bataan and Corregidor soldiers who had been left behind. Mucci told his men that the prisoners would be slaughtered if they didn't act. "You're going to bring out every last man, even if you have to carry them on your backs." His soldiers responded with unbridled enthusiasm, despite the mission's complete lack of strategic sense. This wasn't about strategy; it was about doing what was right.

Coming from Bridgeport, Mucci had a wonderful combination of practicality and flourish. He knew the mission would be one for the ages, so he took along three photographers. However, he also shaved off his stylish pencil mustache as "too damn much trouble." He remained stern and intense as the group marched thirty miles to its destiny in January 1945. Approximately 8,000 Japanese troops jammed the large town of Cabanatuan at this point in the campaign, and this small group of 121 Rangers would be hopelessly outnumbered if they made a mistake. If one of the villages they passed contained a spy or if the Japanese army followed the escape with tanks or planes, they would all die. The men had no special equipment, only the element of surprise.

The Rangers wore no jewelry or metal and used soft caps rather than metal helmets. Mucci inspected them individually to make sure that nothing made noise while they moved. Some carried weapons from the same city as their leader, like the Browning automatic rifle and the new bazookas, produced in Bridgeport for the first time in 1942. Most of the march was through long cogon grass and jungle. On the way, they had to cross a busy

Tales from the Park City

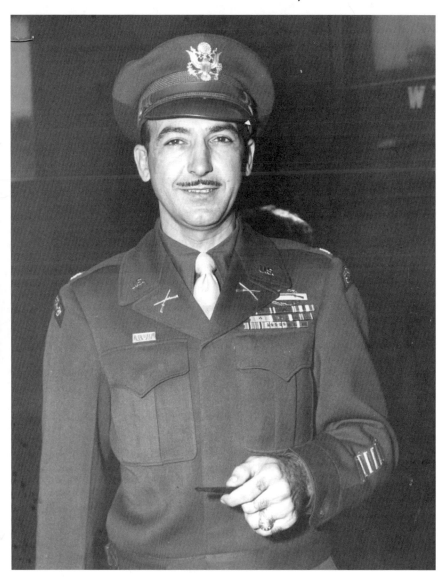

A candid shot of Colonel Henry Mucci with his signature mustache, pipe and grin. *Courtesy of the Bridgeport Public Library Historical Collections.*

road on which the entire Japanese army seemed to be traveling. The Rangers crawled through a ditch under a bridge, one by one.

Near the camp at Cabanatuan, the Alamo Scouts who had joined Mucci's men did their job while the Rangers waited an extra day for the Japanese battalion of eight thousand men to move out of the area. Now they knew

Bridgeport

where the prisoners and Japanese soldiers were positioned, and everyone memorized the maps drawn in the Filipino dirt. Toward evening, they left their positions and crept silently through the nearby barrios. The Filipinos tied the village dogs' mouths shut so they couldn't bark and alert the enemy troops. They gathered water buffalo carts that poor farmers donated for the cause to take the wounded and weak prisoners the thirty miles back to American lines. If only one of the villagers had gossiped or been an informer to the Japanese, the mission would have failed. But no one said a word.

Joined by Filipino guerrillas, the Rangers crawled on their stomachs for the last mile across flat, dry rice paddies that felt as hard and exposed as concrete. An American plane that Mucci called in from the Air Corps buzzed the towers to distract the guards. Mucci's second-in-command, Captain Prince, waited with the main assault unit while F Company crawled to the rear of the camp. Once in position, the shocked assault force heard bells ring out, but it was only a POW clanging the camp time bell. However, at 7:40 p.m. a guard in the tower in the rear saw one of F Company's men and raised the alarm. It was the last thing he ever did, and Mucci's Rangers stormed the compound. Caught in their barracks, most of the Japanese soldiers were shot. At first, the prisoners thought that the massacre had begun and their lives were over. But the monstrous figures strapped with bandoleers quickly let them know that the "Yanks are here."

Resistance began, and the Rangers took scattered rifle fire. Wounded men from the camp were thrown onto litters and carried out by these huge farm boys, suddenly glad of their months of fitness training in New Guinea. The Americans checked every hut and hustled the 513 POWs across the Cabu River while guerrilla forces helped keep off pursuit at the bridge. Only thirty minutes had passed since the first shot was fired. Just two Rangers died, and every prisoner from the camp was freed and brought safely back to the American lines: amazed, grateful and weeping "without shame."

General Douglas MacArthur awarded Mucci the Distinguished Service Cross, promoted him to full colonel and said that the mission was "magnificent." Upon his return, hometown boy Henry was treated as a national hero with a spectacular parade but never gave a single interview about the raid. Despite his earlier tendencies toward grandiosity, he wanted no credit or popularity from his actions. Perhaps saving over five hundred soldiers from certain death had brought out his humble, practical side. Two years later, he married a woman named Marion Fountain and had four children with her. An athlete until the end, he died at age eighty-six after being pounded by huge waves while swimming in the ocean. As Sergeant Vance Shears said of Bridgeport's hero, "We all would have died for him, he was the very best."

Chapter 11

THE *POGO* YEARS

Walt Kelly's family moved to Connecticut when he was only two years old. Like many in the Park City, his family background was mixed; in his case it was Scotch, Irish, English, French and Austrian. Kelly's father worked in one of the munitions plants that was making Bridgeport the nation's arsenal, but he also had a talent for art. He taught his son the power of pictures and even told his family one evening at supper, "Language is the worst means of communication known to man."

Walt's childhood was full of the usual mishaps, like falling into a coal scuttle and braving chickenpox. He fondly remembered incidents such as the time his homemade boat struck a swimming duck in Bunnell's Pond and broke, or the time he was forced to shoot a rabid rabbit. He also suffered more seriously from a strange paralysis on his left side that lasted two years. Those mishaps did not stop Walt from attending Warren Harding High School, where he studied French and, according to him, the French teacher. He worked on the high school newspaper as an editor, a reporter and a cartoonist. He was so good at this that the *Bridgeport Post* asked him to report on the issues that mattered to young people.

Walt stayed on with the *Post* after school, writing about local events, reporting on crime and occasionally drawing cartoons. The newspaper ran a biography of P.T. Barnum, and Kelly illustrated it with glee, enjoying bringing the strange animals and comical situations to life. With a fedora and a cigar, he looked like he belonged in the dingy newsrooms and saloons of Lafayette Street, always rushing to make a deadline. However, the job at the *Post* did not pay well, so he chose to work for the Bridgeport Welfare Department during the early years of the Depression.

Bridgeport itself had chosen a fresh and fascinating solution to this worldwide catastrophe. In 1933, a man named Jasper McLevy ran on the Socialist platform and was swept into office, perhaps helped by Walt Kelly's political cartoon endorsements. The son of two Scotch immigrants, McLevy had been born in 1878, during the heady days of Bridgeport's expansion. He worked in local factories, apprenticed in the roofing trade and finally started his own business. Becoming active in the labor movement and the AFL, he read Edward Bellamy's *Looking Backward* and moved farther left. Beginning his runs for mayor in 1911, he waited patiently twenty-two years for the city to elect him.

As mayor, McLevy immediately instituted a policy of good government reform, cutting corners and slashing expenditures. He instituted a strong civil service program, destroying the old patronage system. He revamped the sewers and cleared old slums for better low-income housing. With unusual control, he cut the $16 million city debt in half, and his frugality became legendary. When the snow piled high in the winter, McLevy was credited with a famous retort to complaints about shoddy plowing: "God put the snow there, let Him take it away." It was probably a misquotation uttered by one of his employees, but it fit the character of this tightfisted leader. Bridgeport immigrants, workers and businessmen all loved him, reelecting him time and time again. He served twenty-four years as mayor until 1957, when he was finally defeated in a largely discredited election by only 161 votes.

Meanwhile, in 1935, Walt Kelly moved to Los Angeles to follow his sweetheart, Helen DeLacey, whom he had met at choir practice in high school. She transferred there as an executive for the Girl Scouts, and he got a job at Walt Disney Studios as an animator, drawing and finishing panels for such films as *Fantasia*, *Dumbo* and *Snow White and the Seven Dwarfs*.

Coincidentally, another Bridgeporter named Adriana Caselotti worked on *Snow White*, lending her voice to the title character. In 1916, Adriana was born to be an opera star. Everyone in her Italian immigrant family in Bridgeport was in the business: her father taught music, her mother sang at the Royal Opera and her sister was a voice teacher who later helped teach Maria Callas. Adriana was only eighteen when she beat out scores of competitors to be the voice of Snow White. Walt Disney had asked her father if any of his students might have the right type of voice but heard Adriana singing and was elated, giving her the role of her dreams. Strangely and unfortunately, her convoluted contract with Disney did not allow her to appear or sing in any other films, and she returned to opera.

Walt Kelly often felt the constraints of working at Disney, as well. In his characteristic three-piece suit, starched collar and bow tie, he trudged through the grunt work at Disney until the strike in 1941, when he refused to take sides, moving back east with Helen, now his wife. During World War II, he illustrated guidebooks and worked as a civilian attaché to the army's

Tales from the Park City

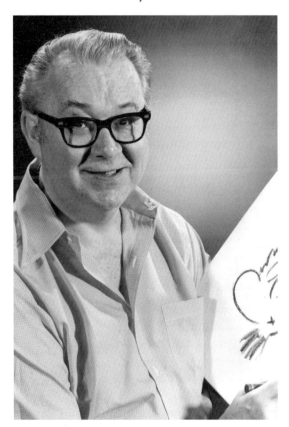

Fellow cartoonist Al Capp noted that Walt Kelly, "when he chooses to be, is one of the funniest men in the world." *Courtesy of the Bridgeport Public Library Historical Collections.*

foreign language unit. Here he encountered the Georgia dialect that would add flavor to the cartoon that would make him famous: *Pogo.*

Pogo developed through the war years and first appeared in Animal Comics. The publication failed, and Walt wanted to know why. With typical Bridgeport gumption, he sought out children and grilled them on what they disliked about it. Their honesty startled him: "That comic book didn't have no action in it. Nobody shot nobody. It was full of mice in red and blue pants. It stunk." Kelly took the advice to heart as he moved to his next career as both art director and political cartoonist for the *New York Star.* In this strange dual capacity, he directed himself to generate a daily comic strip. Then, in 1949, he produced *Pogo Comics*, issue number one. It caught the attention of a few editors throughout the country, and slowly but surely more and more added the strip to their newspapers.

Pogo was an "intellectual" cartoon with a broad appeal, named for its protagonist, a small possum who lived in the Okefenokee Swamp. Kelly called his central character "the reasonably patient, soft-hearted, naïve, friendly little person we all think we are." Living in the swamp were over a hundred other animals, all with their own personalities and manners of speaking. Each was symbolic or allegorical of something in the culture at large. Senator Joe McCarthy became a nasty, cowardly bobcat called Simple J. Malarkey. A cow named Horrors Greeley was modeled after the newspaper magnate who had promoted P.T. Barnum so well during the 1800s. It was part of a new breed of seemingly innocent comics satirizing politics, culture and American life.

By chance, another cartoonist in this movement had ties to Bridgeport. Alfred Caplan was a New Haven boy, but his terrible school performance led him to five years of high school in the Park City. Flunking "plane geometry" for nine terms in a row does not seem like an auspicious start for the creator of another sophisticated cartoon, nor did the nine different art schools that followed. However, eventually he created the popular and satirical *Li'l Abner*, and his fame was made. "Al Capp" kept in touch with his adopted city, though, collaborating with University of Bridgeport students to create his strange and lovable character "the Shmoo." Along with Kelly and a few other pioneers, he helped create comic strips that were full of broad humor but could also be read on another, more serious level.

By 1958, fifty million people enjoyed *Pogo* every day. As Kelly's cartoon became more popular, it also became more political. Pogo himself was put forth as the presidential candidate by Molester Mole and Deacon Mushrat, who actually ran against him, figuring they could easily beat such an innocent. The naïve little possum became a countercultural figure, and college students held rallies to promote "Pogo for President." Buttons with "I Go Pogo" were symbols of anti-establishment political protest throughout the fifties and sixties.

One of the places that these buttons appeared was at the University of Bridgeport, now a thriving campus, adding buildings and students every year. Its seaside campus provided a prominent, strong focus for cultural activity in the city. In 1959, the great bandleader Duke Ellington provided music for the Christmas Ball at the university. Throughout the mid-century, the campus brought poets and musicians of repute to town, from Gwendolyn Brooks and Nikki Giovanni to Aaron Copland and Leonard Bernstein. As it grew in size and stature, it also hosted a wide variety of political figures, such as Malcolm X, Eleanor Roosevelt and Martin Luther King Jr. Mrs. Roosevelt's speech inspired such a huge crowd that it had to be moved downtown to the Klein Memorial Auditorium.

Dr. King was given an honorary degree and gave a lecture on "The American Dream," speaking to over two thousand students and townspeople. He stressed

Tales from the Park City

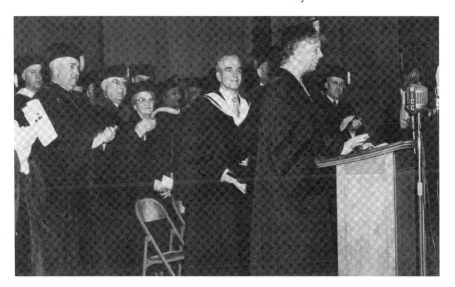

Eleanor Roosevelt gives a speech on the United Nations for the University of Bridgeport in 1953. *Courtesy of the University of Bridgeport Archives.*

the importance of America becoming a truly democratic country and providing equal opportunities for all. "Brotherhood is our only salvation," he insisted, urging the spellbound audience to compassionate action. Two months later, at the 1961 commencement, Dr. King was presented with an honorary doctoral hood. Professor Petitjean read a citation, calling him "a dedicated Christian minister, uncompromising idealist, dreamer of the American dream."

But the university was not the only center of new life for Bridgeport. The entertainment industry was flourishing again, in the form of an amusement park on Pleasure Beach. The beachfront park had been known as Steeplechase Island since 1909, after the owner of Coney Island had bought it. Its name came from a unique, gravity-powered ride, which involved carousel-like horses on metal tracks that participants would sit on and race over a long, undulating course. The city of Bridgeport bought it back in 1919, expanding and improving it.

A long pier that stretched out toward the center of Bridgeport Harbor provided access to the triangular island. When gas rationing went into effect during the war, the Brickerhoff Ferry shuttled excited families from the docks downtown. A breakwater curved from the point of the triangle out to nearly meet another that stretched across from Seaside Park, forming a literal mouth where the ships squeezed into the port. A wooden and later iron swing bridge over the long, sandy causeway allowed eager children to scramble into the park.

Bridgeport

Boardwalks crisscrossed Pleasure Beach, their wooden planks leading eager visitors to huge aerial swings, a shiny carousel and an echoing roller-skating rink. A miniature railroad and a huge roller coaster rushed past the concession stands and restaurant. Lovers plied the backwaters in rowboats or took the ride they called "The Old Mill." At its entrance, the large Dutch windmill belied a scary interior never intended as a tunnel of love. But that never deterred couples from using the cool, aquatic ride to escape the heat of the summer days.

Wearing bobby socks and saddle shoes, teenagers would flock eagerly to the huge dancing pavilion with its glass sides, tall bell towers and flags fluttering in the brisk sea breeze. Inside was the largest ballroom in New England, which glittered with colored lights. Stars like Gene Krupa, Glenn Miller, the Dorsey Brothers, Guy Lombardo and Artie Shaw jammed here, encouraged by the presence of Columbia Records. In 1941, the company pressed close to 100 million records in Bridgeport for luminaries like Louis Armstrong and Leonard Bernstein. Unfortunately, Columbia left Bridgeport in 1964, though the Pavilion continued hosting dances for nine more years, until the extraordinary building was consumed by hungry flames.

Those who could not afford Pleasure Beach often swam in the lake at Beardsley Park, near the icehouse. In the days before refrigerators, the frozen lake would be cut, harvested and kept until summer. From the icehouse, the ice man delivered chunks to neighborhood homes, while children followed, picking up chips of ice that fell from the carriage. Their parents would also send them to the bars with metal pails to fill them with beer. When they grew older, they would buy ice cream at Jean's on East Main Street or slip into the Main Line Diner for a more substantial meal. They would scrounge up the money for the Hippodrome or the American Strand. The more enterprising kids would work the shoe shine stands at the railroad station or on the street corners downtown.

Teenagers sometimes hung out downtown at Café Howard, where swing bands and singers would practice before concerts at the Ritz Ballroom, or sneak drinks at the Pink Elephant in the Barnum Hotel near the train station. Bridgeport native Cecilia Finnell remembers meeting a young man in the Pink Elephant who bought her and her friend Katy Jankura a drink before they walked him to the train station. He told them a far-fetched story about going to drama school. "He was very good looking," she said dreamily. Later, she saw him in a film and realized that his story about being an actor was not a "line." That man was Bridgeport east-ender Robert Mitchum.

Not all the kids were spending their days at the Pink Elephant. Fred DeLuca was only seventeen years old when he opened a sandwich shop in Bridgeport. In 1965, he convinced a friend of the family, Dr. Peter Buck, to loan him the

Tales from the Park City

money to open "Pete's Super Submarines" so he could make enough money to pay for college. But the sandwich shop was so successful that he began to open new stores around New England. The franchise would be called Subway, and would grow to be one of the leading food chains on the planet.

Meanwhile, in the north end of the city, Beardsley Park underwent a transformation. Parks Commissioner Wesley Hayes had long chafed at the idea that Connecticut had no zoo, and he proposed building one on the hill above Bunnell's Pond. At the time, the only tourist attraction in Beardsley Park was the "Anne Hathaway Cottage," a replica of William Shakespeare's home built on the 300th anniversary of his death. So, in 1922, Barnum and Bailey donated flocks of birds and circus retirees to trigger the birth of what would become Connecticut's only zoo. A few years later, $50,000 was pumped into the park to build the greenhouse, where the animals stayed during the winter. During the summer, camels, peacocks, monkeys, deer, llamas and leopards lounged in cages for the public to admire.

At first, visitors could actually drive through the park to see the exhibits without leaving their cars. Open-topped buses would cram with day-trippers ready to tour the city, and the zoo became a cherished stop. Beardsley continued to grow from the 1930s to the 1970s, adding animals and buildings, including a monkey house complete with trees, swings and ropes. Lovely, rose-decked trellises led visitors to the greenhouse, and a terrace on top of the hill became a carousel. The zoo added unusual animals like an albino robin, two silver foxes, tree ducks and eventually an elephant named Shakuntala. She lived there happily for twenty years as Bridgeport's only elephant, unaware that once dozens of her species had roamed the park on their training marches.

Beardsley Park now had a jewel in its crown, and Bridgeport had a magnet to draw excited sightseers from around the entire state. The city had flourished beyond its industrial roots, from a boomtown of mansions and factories to a thriving cultural center. Meanwhile, hometown boy Walt Kelly had become the president of the National Cartoonist Society and was taking the cartoon world by storm with *Pogo*. Not only was the strip commenting on issues of the day, but it was also penetrating into public consciousness. Eschewing his father's advice about language, Kelly stretched and played with English, turning famous quotes on their heads and playfully distorting the slang of the day. When confronted with an ever-growing sea of garbage, the good-hearted possum added to American lingo when he famously observed: "We have met the enemy and he is us."

Hearkening back to his roots, Kelly also invented a new character named P.T. Bridgeport. Obviously a caricature of Phineas Barnum and the less than

Bridgeport

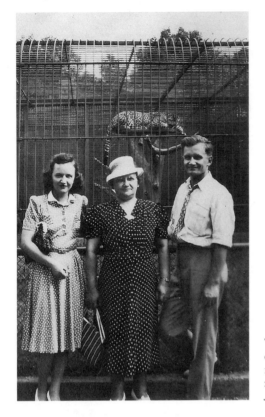

The Beardsley Zoo's exotic animals drew day-trippers from across the region. The Nawrocki family visits the zoo in the late 1930s. *Courtesy of Amy Nawrocki.*

savory aspects of twentieth-century Bridgeport politics, this unlovable bear ran a political circus instead of a literal one. He acted as Pogo's campaign manager, rigged elections and spoke the rhetorical language of someone saying a lot of nothing. This sophistry was displayed in speech balloons printed in clever circus poster type. The Bridgeport bear scratched at fleas, sported a mismatched checkered shirt and striped tie and flourished a cane and top hat. Kelly had come full circle, and the city that had given him his start was now spoofed on the comics page of every newspaper in the country.

Bridgeport was well past its centenary by now and had developed its own thriving culture, which continued to resonate with the American culture at large. But as Kelly's Porky Pine advised the characteristically overwrought Albert the alligator, "Don't take life so serious, son…it ain't *no how* permanent." This unfortunate truth hit Walt Kelly when he had his leg amputated due to diabetes and died shortly afterward on October 18, 1973. The city's prosperity as a cultural and economic center would soon follow, sending it into a tragic tailspin. As Kelly's dramatic bear Phineas T. Bridgeport observed sadly, "Gone is the summer season, the big show ends, the curtain falls…"

Chapter 12

TRAGEDY AND REBIRTH

When locals speak of the fall of Bridgeport in the last decades of the twentieth century, they seldom agree on a date. One might recall fondly a last sip at the tearoom in D.M. Read's, before the 129-year-old department store finally closed. Another might shudder while mentioning the worst construction accident in the history of Connecticut, the collapse of the L'Ambiance Plaza that buried twenty-eight workers. Some mark the 1973 fire that wrecked the ballroom at Pleasure Beach, leaving it a home of plovers, ospreys and parrots. Those who remember with their stomachs point to the long-ago loss of the Frisbie Pie Company, the closing of Soderholm's in 1979 or the shutdown of the last of the wholesale bakeries in 1983. Bridgeporters who prefer symbolism look to the day when the devastating Hurricane Gloria swept through the city. More recently, they shake their heads at the moment that Gutzon Borglum's famous Wheeler Memorial Fountain was struck by a minivan. Was it early, when, in 1981, federal indictments marred the city government and exposed corruption at all levels of the administration? Or was it twenty years later, when, in 2001 the feds charged the mayor with racketeering, extortion and bribery? No one can agree.

What they do agree on is that the last decades of Bridgeport's twentieth century became an American tragedy. Built on manufacturing, the Park City felt the sting of urban industrial flight. Singer, which had taken over the Wheeler and Wilson Company, closed the fabled Bridgeport plant in 1970. The seemingly invulnerable Bridgeport Brass declined throughout the decade, at last firing its 650 employees in 1980. In 1985, the legendary Remington plant, owned by General Electric since 1920, lost a huge government contract. It admitted hazardous waste violations, began moving operations to Arkansas and, a few years later, boxed up the last round of ammunition. Then, Bryant Electric's new owners, Westinghouse, closed the half-million-square-foot plant in 1988. The largest producer of lace in the

Bridgeport

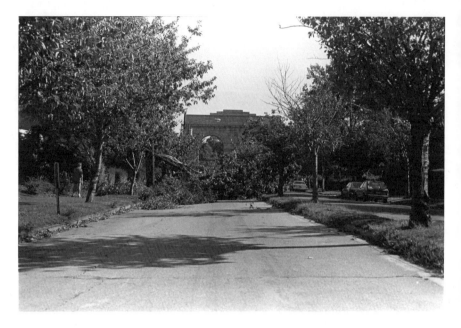

With eighty-mile-per-hour winds, Hurricane Gloria hit Bridgeport in September 1985, felling trees like this one on Park Avenue in front of the Perry Arch. *Courtesy of the University of Bridgeport Archives.*

country, the American Fabrics Company, closed its Bridgeport factory with the decade. Carpenter Steel, Bullards and Mechanics and Farmers Bank perished. With no clients, other businesses that depended on manufacturing left the metropolitan limits. Built on the seemingly strong foundations of industry, the city became vulnerable to its loss.

At the University of Bridgeport, things progressed no better. When the baby boomers and Vietnam veterans finished school, enrollment waned. One third of the fifty buildings on campus emptied. A *60 Minutes* special focusing on the city's crime rate and drug problem led hundreds of enrolled students to leave. Then, when the administration decided to cut wages and fire tenured faculty in 1990, the teachers went on strike. The city already had a bad history with teacher strikes. A bitter public school strike in 1978 resulted in 279 teachers jailed when they defied court order. The professors at the university had walked off the job four times since then, but this would be much worse. In fact, it became the longest faculty strike in United States history, leading to the school's near ruin.

While the university remained at the brink, the city itself teetered on the edge of financial ruin. Mary Moran had become the city's first female mayor and tried to solve the city's problems by filing for bankruptcy. This

Tales from the Park City

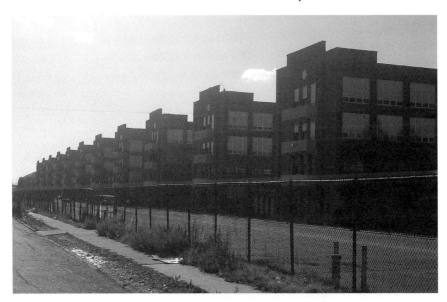

Above: Today, the Remington Arms/GE factory sits largely abandoned in north Bridgeport. *Courtesy of the author.*

Right: The three-year dispute at the already strained University of Bridgeport became the longest faculty strike in U.S. history. *Courtesy of the University of Bridgeport Archives.*

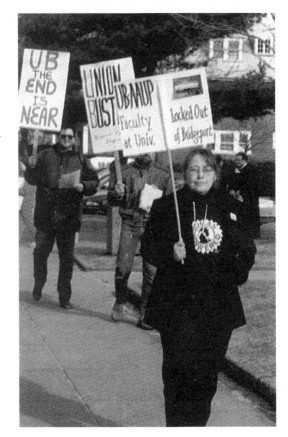

plan backfired, scaring off investors and earning Bridgeport the dubious distinction of being the nation's first major city to go to bankruptcy court. Construction projects shut down and banks refused to lend the city money. Moran's replacement, Joseph Ganim, heroically appeared to put the city on the right track, until the federal authorities put him in prison.

Such a string of tragedies would be enough to send another community into total ruin. But in this town of dreamers and pioneers, hope endured during those dark years. Stalwart institutions like the People's United Bank, founded in 1842, kept going strong as the largest regional bank with headquarters in New England. A few promising projects achieved success, like the harbor destination of Captain's Cove Seaport. The annual Barnum Festival, started in 1949 to take workers' minds off the falling postwar economy, served the same purpose through these dark days. The scientific Discovery Museum challenged city children to think beyond their present lives. And Shakespearean plays filled Beardsley Park, as they had since 1916, with "tongues in trees, books in the running brooks, sermons in stones, and good in everything."

In a world of lost chances, Bridgeport got back some of its own when, in the late 1980s, one of the Wham-O co-founders admitted that they lifted their name from the Frisbie Pie Company. A ten-inch Frisbie pie tin went into the Smithsonian Museum. And though an unconditional contract with the Wright brothers prevents the Smithsonian from ever admitting the possibility that Gustave Whitehead flew his plane before them, local science teacher Andrew Kosch proved that it could have been done when he flew a replica of Number 21 on December 29, 1986. Another replica was successfully flown in Germany in 1997, and serious debate continued on the Park City's place in the history of flight.

Behind the scenes, almost unnoticed by those mourning the loss of old Bridgeport, the conversion into something new began. Some factories were torn down while others were transformed. Lofts went up in the old Warner Brothers factory and condominiums filled the Columbia Records Building. Local artists breathed new life into the American Fabrics Company, Read's Department Store and a sector of old Remington Arms. The neighborhood of Black Rock started a renewal revolution, opening coffee bars, fine restaurants and stylish shops. Yacht clubs, markets and a vibrant arts center created a new, eclectic population dedicated to building the community. Concerned citizens restored the Black Rock Lighthouse in 1998 and relit it two years later, paying homage to the hard work of Catherine Moore.

The twenty-first century continued to prompt effort and innovation. Built on the site of the Jenkins Valve Factory from 1998 to 2001, the Harbor Yard

Tales from the Park City

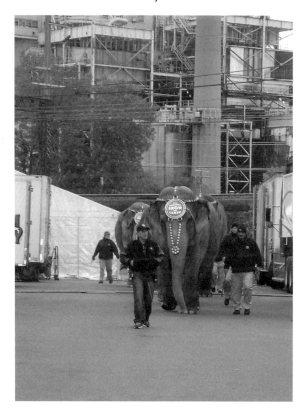

Elephants from the Ringling Brothers and Barnum and Bailey Circus walk in front of the enormous United Illuminating power plant in 2008. *Courtesy of Lorraine Galow.*

entertainment complex immediately drew crowds from around the state. The arena hosted the hometown hockey team, the Sound Tigers, and the ballpark hosted the Atlantic League baseball team, the Bridgeport Bluefish. Set between the railroad tracks and the United Illuminating plant, Harbor Yard also became the site of ceremonies, concerts and the circus, bringing Ringling Brothers and Barnum and Bailey back to town.

A new state-of-the-art bus terminal relayed tourists in to see Charles Stratton's miniature carriage at the Barnum Museum and musical extravaganzas at the renovated Downtown Cabaret. The Playhouse on the Green continued a strong community theatre tradition in its latest home on McLevy Green, and the Gathering of the Vibes music and art festival swarmed over Seaside Park for three days every summer, bringing thousands of energized campers to the broad green lawns. In 2007 and 2008, a restaurant boom released pizzerias and French bistros on the delighted populace. And the Housatonic Community College Museum of Art continued to assemble the largest collection of any American two-year college, boasting works by artists like Rodin, Matisse, Picasso, Chagall and Ansel Adams.

Bridgeport

Farther down Lafayette Street, after struggling throughout the 1990s, the reborn University of Bridgeport grew faster than any other college in New England. Thousands of international students from ninety-one countries thronged to the campus, quite at home in this city built by immigrants, filling the once empty dormitories and streets and bringing the south side of the city to life. The fabled Fones School cleaned the city's teeth in a new multimillion-dollar facility, the proud progenitor of more than 200 dental hygiene schools and 120,000 registered dental hygienists in the United States.

The future will no doubt hold even more changes. A new Black Rock Library will soon open and take its place with the Burroughs Library as part of one of the best urban library systems in the country. Pleasure Beach may be sold to the United States Department of the Interior and turned into a National Wildlife Refuge. A train depot in Black Rock might finally give it the connections to the world it always needed. A monument honoring World War II soldiers could be established in Veteran's Memorial Park. And, most encouragingly, sites along the Pequonnock River and at Steel Point prime for billion-dollar projects, perhaps set to turn the city's waterfront property into a mix of affordable housing and luxury condominiums.

Nevertheless, the strength of Bridgeport never dwelled in billion-dollar projects; it lives in the people and their stories. And every year more join the anthology of the future, in dozens of languages, by immigrants from lands like Lebanon and Portugal, Korea and Cambodia. We could listen to the chronicles of the Chaves Bakery, which took the oven mitts from Frisbie to raise a booming baking business in the city and beyond. Children might gather around to wonder at the story of how the Beardsley Zoo keepers bred Siberian tigers and South American ocelots. And we would find dozens of fascinating librettos at the Klein Auditorium, where a world-class symphony plays, led by renowned maestro Gustav Meier. Who knows what tales this twenty-first century will bring to the Park City? What innovations and inventions brew right now at the tables of Ralph and Rich's or the Acoustic Café? What American dreams whisper under the sycamores of Washington Park?

Driving along the Colonel Henry Mucci Highway into the heart of the city, you can almost hear these hidden futures speak. You can hear them echo from the hall where Abraham Lincoln gave his campaign speech, off each brick of Cesar A. Batalla School and in the songs of the enigmatic green parrots that somehow thrive in Seaside Park. They speak of the mysterious power of the possible, which has guided the people of Bridgeport through every transformation. They tell us that our fears are unfounded, that invention always triumphs and that human achievement follows the industry of hope. They tell us that these tales from the Park City will be written by generations yet to come.

BIBLIOGRAPHY

"Abraham Lincoln and Connecticut." The Lincoln Institute. Abraham Lincoln's Classroom. http://www.abrahamlincolnsclassroom.org.

Allen, William F. *The Miracle at Seaside Park: A History of the University of Bridgeport to 1974*. Bridgeport, CT: University of Bridgeport, 1974.

American Experience. "People & Events: Henry Mucci and the Rangers." 2003. PBS Online. http://www.pbs.org.

Axelrod, David. *Bataan Rescue*. Film. PBS: American Experience, 2003.

Barnum, Phineas T. *The Colossal P.T. Barnum Reader*. Edited by James W. Cook. Urbana: University of Illinois Press, 2005.

Becker, Stephen. *Comic Art in America*. New York: Simon and Schuster, 1959.

Boston Transcript. "An Airship Partnership." August 19, 1901. Gustave Whitehead's Flying Machines. www.gustavewhitehead.org.

Brandon, Ruth. *A Capitalist Romance*. Philadelphia: J.B. Lippincott Company, 1977.

Bridgeport Herald. "Connecticut Junior College Will Open Here." January 22, 1928.

Bridgeport Life. "Connecticut Junior College." January 29, 1927.

Bibliography

———. "Joseph 'Pious' Frisbie Speaks at Kiwanis." February 7, 1925.

Bridgeport Light. "The Best Built Car in America." August 16, 1989.

Bridgeport Post. "Bridgeport Man's First Automobile Ran on Cellar Floor of Home...Built at 16." April 17, 1927.

———. "Cliffe Expects Never To See Seaside Regain Former Beauty." October 14, 1938.

———. "General W.H. Noble Dead." January 18, 1894.

———. "It's Doughnuts to Dollars in Bradbury's Life." November 23, 1933.

———. "The Junior College Idea." January 18, 1927.

———. "Singer Company Shuts December 1." October 30, 1970.

———. "Surgeon's World Calls Fairfield Girl." September 7, 1933.

Bridgeport Standard. "The Sea Side Park." January 15, 1867.

Bridgeport Sunday Post. "Junior College Head Lauded for Preliminary School Work." March 15, 1936.

———. "Pioneer Automobile Builder Recalls His Early Motor Driving Experiences." April 22, 1928.

———. "Production Line Bakery Saves Ma the Job of Making Pie." November 5, 1939.

———. "WPA Debunks Story of Barnum Giving City Seaside Park." April 24, 1938.

Bridgeport Telegram. "Cortright Gives Talk on New Deal." September 20, 1933.

———. "Junior College of Connecticut to Be Dedicated Tonight." February 24, 1928.

Bibliography

———. "Mayor Gives Talk at Junior College." December 12, 1933.

———. "Simon Lake Gives Talk to Students on Early Studies." April 27, 1928.

"Bridgeport Working: Voices from the 20th Century." Bridgeport Public Library Historical Collections Department. http://www.bridgeporthistory.org.

Bucki, Cecelia. "Dilution and Craft Tradition: Munitions Workers in Bridgeport, Connecticut, 1915–1919." *The New England Working Class and the New Labor History*. Edited by Herbert G. Graham and Donald H. Bell. Urbana: University of Illinois Press, 1987: 137–56.

Burgeson, John. "Pleasure Beach Now Just a Memory." *Connecticut Post*, May 25, 2008.

Burr, Nelson. *Abraham Lincoln: Western Star over Connecticut*. Farmington, CT: Lithographics, Inc., 1984.

Chevon, Harry. "There's No Call to Arms: Bridgeport Era Ends at Closing of Remington." *Post-Telegram*, December 17, 1989.

Christoffersen, John. "Bridgeport Mayor Guilty on 16 Counts in Federal Corruption Trial." Associated Press, March 19, 2003.

Clifford, Mary Louise, and J. Candance Clifford. *Women Who Kept the Lights*. Williamsburg, VA: Cypress Communications, 1993.

Cochrane, Dorothy, Von Hardesty and Russell Lee. *The Aviation Careers of Igor Sikorsky*. Seattle: University of Washington Press, 1989.

Cole, Dale, ed. "The Seventeenth Connecticut Volunteer Infantry." http://home.att.net/~DogSgt/Seventeenth.html.

Collier, Christopher. *The Pride of Bridgeport: Men and Machines in the Nineteenth Century*. Bridgeport, CT: Museum of Art, Science and Industry, 1979.

Corey, Herbert. *Submarine: The Autobiography of Simon Lake*. New York: D. Appleton-Century Company, Inc., 1938.

Bibliography

Danbury Times. "Talks about New College." 1931.

Danenberg, Elsie Nicholas. *The Story of Bridgeport*. Bridgeport, CT: Bridgeport Centennial, 1936.

Demattia, Robin. *Connecticut's Beardsley Zoo*. Bridgeport, CT: Connecticut Zoological Society, 2002.

Diamond, Jeff. "Arms to Art: Old Remington Factory Houses Artists in a New Role." *Connecticut Post*, June 16, 2000.

Entremont, Jeremy. *The Lighthouses of Connecticut*. Beverly, MA: Commonwealth Editions, 2005.

Epstein, Vicki J. "Write-off Kills Bridgeport Brass." *Bridgeport Post*, January 29, 1985, 25.

Fassett, John D. *UI: History of an Electric Company*. New Haven, CT: The United Illuminating Company, 1990.

Field, John W. *Fig Leaves and Fortunes, a Fashion Company Named WARNACO*. West Kennebunk, ME: Phoenix Publishing, 1990.

Fones, Alfred. *Dental Items of Interest to the Citizens of Bridgeport*. Dental Department of Bridgeport.

Fraser, Bruce. "Connecticut, 1865–1929: An Industrial Society." Connecticut Heritage Gateway. http://www.ctheritage.org.

Glenn, Taylor. "Books and Authors." *Bridgeport Post*, August 27, 1950.

Gordon, Jane. "High Hopes for Bridgeport." *New York Times*, April 22, 2008.

Grimaldi, Lennie. *Only in Bridgeport, 2000: An Illustrated History of the Park City*. Redding, CT: Harbor Communications, Inc., 2000.

Harper's Weekly. "The Housatonic Railroad Slaughter." September 2, 1865.

Harris, Neil. *Humbug: The Art of P.T. Barnum*. Boston: Little, Brown, and Company, 1973.

Bibliography

Hornstein, Harold. "Noble Avenue Bears a Proud Name; Civil War Hero, City's Benefactor." *Bridgeport Sunday Post*, May 29, 1960.

Hurd, D. Hamilton, ed. *History of Fairfield County, Connecticut*. Philadelphia: J.W. Lewis and Co., 1881.

Johnson, Stancil. *Frisbee: A Practitioner's Manual and Definitive Treatise*. New York: Workman Publishing Company, 1975.

Jones, Dick, et al. *Black Rock: A Bicentennial Picture Book*. Bridgeport, CT: Black Rock Civic and Business Men's Club, Inc., 1976.

Judson, George. "Bridgeport Bankruptcy Plea Focuses on Solvency Dispute." *New York Times*, July 24, 1991.

Kelly, Walt. "An Autobiography by the Creator of *Pogo*." Walt Kelly's Pogo. 1954. http://www.pogopossum.com.

Kohut, Jeff. "A Plea to Preserve 'The Woods.'" *Connecticut Post*, June 2, 2002.

Kornfield, Benjamin. "Locomobile Plant Built 40 Ton Tank as Last War Ended." *Bridgeport Sunday Post*, January 4, 1942.

Kunhardt, Phillip, Jr., Phillip B. Kunhardt III and Peter W. Kunhardt. *P.T. Barnum: America's Greatest Showman*. New York: Alfred A. Knopf, 1995.

Lane, Robert. *A Political History of Connecticut during the Civil War*. Washington, D.C.: Catholic University Press, 1941.

Magnell, Denise. "Bryant Shell—Wealth of Memories." *Connecticut Post*, April 19, 1995.

Maher, Kathleen. *A Celebration of the American Spirit in Bridgeport*. Bridgeport, CT: Barnum Museum, 2002.

Malafonte, Victor A. *The Complete Book of Frisbee: The History of the Sport and the First Official Price Guide*. Edited by F. Davis Johnson. Alameda, CA: American Trends Publishing Co., 1998.

BIBLIOGRAPHY

Marshall, Richard. *America's Great Comic-Strip Artists.* New York: Stewart, Tabori, and Chang, 1997.

Maxim, Hiram. *Artificial and Natural Flight.* London: Whittaker and Co., 1915.

May, Earl Chapin. *Century of Silver, 1847–1947, Connecticut Yankees and a Noble Metal.* New York: Rovert M. McBride and Company, 1947.

McCarthy, Mabel. "Dr. Alfred C. Fones: The Father of Dental Hygiene." *Journal of the American Dental Hygienists' Association*: 17–31.

Newman, Irene. Interview. Dental Hygienists' Association. August 31, 1955.

New York Herald. "Inventors in Partnership to Solve Problem of Aerial Navigation." August 19, 1901. Gustave Whitehead's Flying Machines. http://www.gustavewhitehead.org.

New York Times. "Luzon Rescue Hero Silent On Exploits." February 2, 1945, 11.

Niven, John. *Connecticut for the Union.* New Haven, CT: Yale University Press, 1965.

Noble, William Henry, ed. *17th Connecticut Volunteers at Gettysburg: June 30th, and July 1st, 2d, and 3d, 1884.* Bridgeport, CT: The Standard Association Printers, 1884.

Olson, John W. "William B. Hincks: An Army Grunt and Civil War Hero." *Hometown Publications*, November 25, 2005.

Orcutt, Samuel. *A History of the Old Town of Stratford and the City of Bridgeport.* Fairfield, CT: Fairfield County Historical Society, 1886.

Page, Charles D. *History of the Fourteenth Regiment, Connecticut Volunteer Infantry.* Meriden, CT: Horton Printing Co., 1906.

Palmquist, David. *A Pictorial History of Bridgeport.* Norfolk, VA: Donning Company, 1985.

Bibliography

"Pro Patria." Civil War Monuments of Connecticut. Connecticut Historical Society. http://www.chs.org.

Randolph, Stella. *Lost Flights of Gustave Whitehead*. Washington, D.C.: Places, Inc., 1937.

Ravo, Nick. "Education; Faculty Strike Clouds Future at Bridgeport." *New York Times*, September 19, 1990.

Romaine, Merlie. *General Tom Thumb and his Lady*. Taunton, MA: William S. Sullwold Publishing, 1976.

Saxon, A.H. *P.T. Barnum: The Legend and the Man*. New York: Columbia University Press, 1989.

Scientific American. "Experiments with Motor-driven Aeroplanes." September 19, 1903. Gustave Whitehead's Flying Machines. http://www.gustavewhitehead.org.

———. "A New Flying Machine." June 8, 1901. Gustave Whitehead's Flying Machines. http://www.gustavewhitehead.org.

Sides, Hampton. *Ghost Soldiers: The Epic Account of World War II's Greatest Rescue Mission*. New York: Anchor Books, 2002.

"Soldiers' Monument." Civil War Monuments of Connecticut. Connecticut Historical Society. http://www.chs.org.

Stave, Bruce M. "The Great Depression and Urban Political Continuity: Bridgeport Chooses Socialism." *Socialism and the Cities*. Edited by Bruce M. Stave. Port Washington, NY: Kennikat Press, 1975, 157–83.

Thomas, Robert McG., Jr. "Henry A. Mucci Dies at 88; Rescued Survivors of Bataan." *New York Times*, April 24, 1997, D29.

Times-Star. "Dr. Fones Stricken." March 16, 1938.

Waldo, George Curtis. *The Standard's History of Bridgeport*. Bridgeport, CT: Standard Association, 1897.

Bibliography

Walsh, Charles. "Whitehead's Fans Keep Alive Story of Fairfield Flight." *Connecticut Post*, December 14, 2002.

Weider, Stanley. "Dr. Alfred C. Fones." *Dental Students Magazine* (March 1951).

Westmorland, Avril. "Bombay Baking Co, 55 Years Old, Closes." *Bridgeport Post*, April 18, 1983.

Witkowski, Mary. *Bridgeport at Work*. Charleston, SC: Arcadia Publishing, 2002.

———. "Solderholm's Was Known for Swedish Rye Bread." *Bridgeport News*, March 2, 1995.

Yardley, Jonathan. "Pogo, Never Really Gone." *Washington Post*, May 23, 2005.

ABOUT THE AUTHOR

Eric D. Lehman has taught literature and creative writing for over a decade at the University of Bridgeport. He is a senior lecturer and president of the Bridgeport chapter of Phi Kappa Phi. His essays, reviews, poems and stories have been published in dozens of journals and magazines. Travel writing is his passion, whether hiking the Inca Trail in Peru or fly-fishing the rivers of Connecticut.

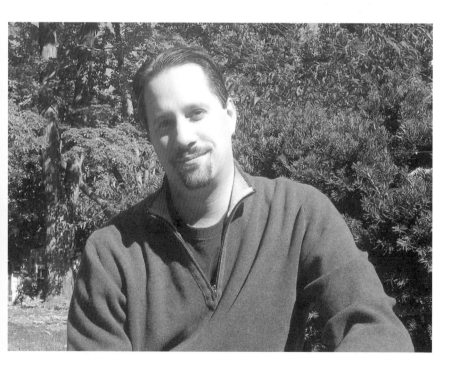

Visit us at
www.historypress.net